Experiments in Art and Capitalism

Volume I

Artful Objects: Graham Harman on Art and the Business of Speculative Realism

Experiments in Art and Capitalism Volume I

Artful Objects: Graham Harman on Art and the Business of Speculative Realism

Contributions by Daniel Birnbaum, Marcia Cavalcante, Micael Dahlen, Pierre Guillet de Monthoux, Graham Harman, Jenny Lantz, Isak Nilson, Sigrid Sandström, Ebba Sjögren, Emma Stenström, Lars Strannegård, Sven-Olov Wallenstein, Jo Widoff, Erik Wikberg

Edited by Isak Nilson and Erik Wikberg

Stockholm School of Economics
Sternberg Press

What Is an Object?

Thirteen Questions about the Object to Graham Harman

Appendix

PREFACE: Object-Oriented Philosophy Brings the Artworks Back In

Some events are quite peculiar. On January 15, 2015, a thousand art students, business scholars, philosophers, and curators made their way through the snow up to the entrance of Moderna Museet in Stockholm. Seldom had so many visited a single lecture on the museum's premises, which, on that evening, was jam-packed. What, then, caused this surge of people up the slopes of Skeppsholmen? What was behind these record audience numbers? Rather than a celebrity or famous artist, a philosopher, who has pushed the development of object-oriented philosophy and speculative realism, took the stage.

The event, a collaboration between Moderna Museet and Stockholm School of Economics, took place at the end of the exhibition "Sculpture after Sculpture," featuring the artists Katharina Fritsch, Jeff Koons, and Charles Ray. The distinguished speaker was the philosopher Graham Harman, who was invited to give a lecture on what an object is from an ontological point of view and the relation between object-oriented philosophy and the arts. The auditorium was so full that some had to follow the seminar from a large screen in an adjoining room.

After the lecture, a symposium followed in the exhibition hall. Among the thirteen sculptures in the hall—depicting everything from a balloon dog, a tractor, and a real-size green elephant erected on a tall podium—thirteen people from Moderna Museet, the Royal Institute of Art, Södertörn University, and Stockholm School of Economics posed thirteen questions about the role of the object in philosophy, art, and business administration.

Ontology and epistemology are two basic concepts in the philosophy of science. Ontology is simply the philosophy of what exists. Epistemology is, just as simply put, the philosophy of how we can gain knowledge about what exists. What makes a conversation about ontology particularly suitable for interdisciplinary gatherings is that all kinds of scientific truth claims, regardless of discipline, require that we first understand their points of departure. Before we can say whether something is true or not, we must first know what exists and how to gain knowledge about it.

The idea behind this publication is to reproduce Harman's lecture as well as the questions and answers from the symposium in its entirety. The book can be read as an introduction to object-oriented philosophy and its consequences for various scientific disciplines. Overall, it discusses everything from whether objects can be traumatized to whether commercial values change the aesthetic qualities of an art object. The book is introductory in character because, rather than providing definitive, exhaustive answers, it opens up continuing philosophical explorations.

From the point of view of the School of Economics, there were several purposes of the arrangement. It was partly about breaking up the academy's disciplinary silo thinking to create a truly interdisciplinary meeting between curators, artists, philosophers, and business scholars. It was also about getting academics out of their teaching and seminar rooms and meeting the interested public.

However, the main purpose of this event for the Stockholm School of Economics was to approach artworks as objects. Business studies of cultural production tend to reduce works of art to prices and price developments or focus on all the social processes that arise in the organizational field in which artworks are embedded. We believe that both of these approaches disregard what is most important—namely, the actual works of art—and we wanted the Moderna Museet seminar to be a first step in redirecting the focus.

Art history and business administration have the common genealogy of often borrowing from other scientific disciplines—and frequently from philosophy. It is by no means a coincidence that one of the more influential texts for art history and organizational theory is philosopher Arthur Danto's article "The Artworld" from 1964.[1] Danto believes that art is what the art world can get away with exhibiting as art. What is perceived as art in the eyes of the art world is what is art, irrespective of the inner qualities of the object.

This has led organizational theorists grounded in sociology to study the organizational fields of artworks and the outside world, rather than the objects themselves. This is in no way an incorrect perspective, but we believe that future research, in tune with both aesthetic and material turns in social science, can be developed by, instead, placing the artworks in the foreground.

How could this be done in practice? After the Moderna Museet seminar, we initiated a project at the Stockholm School of Economics called “Economic Ekphrasis.” *Ekphrasis* is a literary description of a real or fictitious work of art, and *economic ekphrasis* is then defined as “a literary description of or commentary on a visual work of art as a research-educational method in the social and economic sciences.”[2] The seminar, in its limited but eclectic form, was a decisive factor in the latter project coming about.

The seminar with Harman showed that this kind of interdisciplinary meeting with art as the main focus is not merely an academic matter but also concerns a far wider circle. An important aspect of Harman's school of thought is that objects should not be subjected to overmining or undermining. They should neither be reduced to their components nor to their effects. Instead, by seeing artworks as objects and nothing else, we can give business research on art a new direction—where the artworks are, once again, put into focus.

Isak Nilson Erik Wikberg

1 Arthur Danto, “The Artworld,” *Journal of Philosophy* 61, no. 19 (1964): 571–84.
2 Pierre Guillet de Monthoux and Erik Wikberg, eds., *Economic Ekphrasis: Goldin+Senneby and Art for Business Education* (Berlin: Sternberg Press, 2021).

What Is an Object?

Lecture by Graham Harman at Moderna Museet

Thanks to all of you for coming, and a special thanks to those who are sitting in the adjoining room watching the video feed. I am sorry you couldn't get in. This will be my second lecture in Stockholm, and the first was just a few hours ago at Stockholm School of Economics, so I am still pretty fresh to this city. As for the title, I never actually gave a title for this lecture, but they've announced "What Is an Object?" as the title for the entire event, and that's fine. I'll take that as my title here tonight as well.

What is an object? In the art world, especially, there are certain connotations that the word "object" has—often referring to solid physical objects as opposed to performances, Conceptual art, or other things that aren't as physical as an art object is usually taken to be. My sense of the term "object" is much broader than this. Being a philosopher, philosophers have to talk about everything, and "object" is simply the term I use to refer to everything that, in some way, exists, including fictional and imaginary things. So, for me, an object is not necessarily durable. It's not necessarily natural, as opposed to artificial. It's not necessarily simple.

An object, for me, is simply something that cannot be reduced in either of two directions. And reductionism, reducing a thing to something else and thereby losing it, actually happens in two directions. The kind that we normally talk about is when you reduce a thing by explaining the tiny pieces of which it's made. This is what the sciences have taught us how to do very well. It's what the pre-Socratic philosophers were also doing early on at the beginning of Western philosophy and science: telling us that everything is made of water, everything is made of air, everything is made of air, earth, fire, and water mixed together, and so forth. For me, that's not what objects are.

Objects might also come in medium size, or large size, and still be objects. There is nothing privileged about the tiny layer of explanation. There are objects of all sizes in the cosmos. But there is another direction in which people reduce things, and that is the direction of reducing things upward. This involves reducing things by saying objects aren't too *shallow* to be the truth, but are too *deep* to be the truth. We don't need objects, this method says. We simply need relations, or effects, or language, or power, or perceptions, and there is no real object hiding behind any of these. Everything is simply on the surface of the world rather than at the bottom. I will argue against both of these strategies tonight. I will say that we need a new concept of the object, and that this concept brings philosophy and the arts very close together. Arts and design actually, since architecture is another area where I have been working more and more lately.

All right, let me start with "The Third Table," since this is an essay some of you may have read.[1] This was my contribution to the catalogue for documenta three years ago in Kassel. "The Third Table" refers to Sir Arthur Stanley Eddington, the British physicist who is probably best known, surely best known, for his observations of an eclipse that helped to verify Einstein's theory of general relativity. Einstein's theory of gravity entailed a prediction that starlight should move as it passes near the sun. There should be a gravitational effect on the starlight, unlike in Newton's theory. Eddington's observations demonstrated that Einstein was right, and this was the moment when Einstein became a household name—he had already been known for fourteen or so years among scientists, but this was the moment when he became a public figure: the man who had overthrown Newton.

Eddington is also famous, or was famous for quite some time, for the opening image of his Gifford Lectures.[2] Philosophers used to talk about this a lot, but not quite as much anymore. At the beginning of these Gifford Lectures in Scotland, Eddington explained that he was sitting down to write at his table, but it was actually two tables. The second table is the scientific table. It's mostly empty space; it's made up of particles and fundamental fields whirling around and only seems solid. And that's the real table for Eddington, since he is a physicist. But he says there is also another table, which is the practical table. It is the table that's

1 Graham Harman, "The Third Table," in *The Book of Books*, ed. Carolyn Christov-Bakargiev (Ostfildern: Hatje Cantz, 2012), 540–42.
2 Arthur Stanley Eddington, *The Nature of the Physical World* (New York: MacMillan, 1929).

hard, that he can lean on, that he can move around the room, that has a specific price, that has a social history, and so forth. And Eddington concedes that this first table also exists, and it's very hard to get rid of. Of course, as a physicist, he is convinced that the second table is the most real one. But the two will always go hand in hand. We will always be seeing double, the first and second table.

Now, it occurred to me as I was writing this essay for documenta that neither of those tables is the real one. There's actually a third table in between the two that's the real table, and I think I can demonstrate this pretty easily. One way to demonstrate this is to say, first, that a table obviously needs particles in order to exist. I don't think any one of us would think there can be an immaterial table that can separate from its physical substratum and float around by itself. I wouldn't argue for that. But obviously, you could remove a certain number of particles from the table. You could even remove a leg and replace it with another leg, you could change the color of the table, and so forth, and yet it's still, in some sense, the same table. There is an *emergence* of the table over and above the tiny little components that make it up. You can't get rid of them all, but you can get rid of a lot of them without changing the table.

Someone told me once that the atoms in our bodies are recycled on average every seven years. So, the last time I was in Stockholm, in 2005, none of these atoms were here in my body. They were in food, or somewhere else. But you would still call this the same body. It has aged ten years since then, but it is still my body as it was in 2005. And so, there's a sense in which this second table cannot account for the emergence of things over and above their ultimate components, and as Manuel DeLanda has shown in his book *A New Philosophy of Society*, a lot of times there are objects that can create their own parts or replace them.[3]

An example would be the city of Stockholm. I don't think it's ridiculous to say that, in some sense, this is the same city as the one of Gustavus Adolphus. True, no one is here today who was there in his time. There is one ship that we saw at the museum yesterday that may date from this time. But it's not convincing to say that this is a different Stockholm every time someone is born or dies, or every time a hair falls off somebody's head. This would be a very arbitrary philosophy, in which we would be saying that Stockholm is no more than a nickname for all the positions of all the atoms at any given moment. Of course, that changes constantly, but there is still something about Stockholm that remains.

All right, so that's the problem with the second table. What about the first, practical table? Well, the problem with the first table—the practical thing that has a certain position in the world at any given moment—is as follows: I can move the table around. I can paint it. I can sell it to somebody. I can ship it to another continent. And it's still, in some sense, the same table. So, the first table also does not get at the root of the issue. There's a third table in between the first two. And only because there's a third table, does the first table make any sense. Only because there's a third table that can be moved into different positions is it possible to move it to a new position without changing it into something different. A table is not just what it is at any given moment; it's something more than that. It's a surplus beyond its current state in the world. You can move it around, just like you can with any other object, and it's still the same object, just like you can replace some of the atoms or even some pieces of the table and it's still the same table.

What's so important about this is that we see a lot of philosophies today that are very geared toward a relational approach to the world. They are largely reacting against the old substance idea, or assuming that there are simply hard physical objects out there, and then we accidentally put them in certain positions. There has been a reaction against that to such an extreme that the relational view of philosophy has almost taken over the world. And if you look at contemporary continental philosophy, you are going to see a lot of people saying that individual objects are not primary, that there are individuating processes that come before that, that are more primary than the table.[4]

You are going to see a different sort of critique of substance from Bruno Latour, my favorite living philosopher, whom I, nonetheless, disagree with strongly on this point. Latour thinks a thing is nothing more than what it *does*. An object is whatever it transforms, modifies, perturbs, or creates.[5] That is why he calls it an actor and not an object: what an actor does is act, whereas, for me, an object is always something more than any of its actions right now because these actions can be changed and it would still be the same object, within certain limits. So, this is what object-oriented philosophy is about: looking for third tables, third electrons, third musical instruments, or third cities. It's about looking for whatever there is in a thing that is not reducible to its components or to its effects.

3 Manuel DeLanda, *A New Philosophy of Society: Assemblage Theory and Social Complexity* (London: Continuum, 2006).
4 See, for example, Gilbert Simondon, *L'individuation à la lumière des notions de forme et d'information* (Grenoble: Jérôme Millon, 2005).
5 Bruno Latour, *Pandora's Hope: Essays on the Reality of Science Studies* (Cambridge, MA: Harvard University Press, 1999), 122.

Now, there's a problem with this, which is that all knowledge that we know of involves one of those two kinds of reductions.[6] If somebody asks you to explain what something is, there are basically two possible kinds of answers you can give. You can tell them what it's made of, or you can tell them what it does. If someone asks me what a certain solution is in the glass [*pointing at a glass of water*], I can say that this is H_2O, or I can say it's a thirst-quencher. Those are the only two kinds of knowledge we have, whereas I am trying to say that the object itself, the water itself, is somewhere in between those two explanations.

Those explanations are parasitical on the water itself. And, for this reason, in object-oriented philosophy, it turns out to be the case that philosophy is not a kind of knowledge. No, philosophy is not a knowledge. Philosophy is something more than and less than a knowledge. Now, having said that, it's actually not such an original idea because I would claim that this is exactly what Socrates was talking about when he talked about *philosophia*. Philosophy, philosophia, means love of wisdom, not wisdom. It was the Sophists who claimed to have wisdom. They were the ones who took money to teach you the truth of things, and that truth was pretty minimal. The truth was that everything is true, or that nothing is true, and that, therefore, you should simply know how to win arguments. This is what they would teach young people to do, whereas Socrates is the one who never attains knowledge about anything.

Socrates is famous for asking the definitions of things in his conversations. It's often forgotten that he never reaches any such definitions: no Platonic dialogue ends with an answer about what justice is, or virtue is, or what friendship is, or what love is. These are always left hanging in the air. Any particular answer turns out to be inadequate. Another way of saying this is that you cannot *paraphrase* objects. This term comes from literary criticism of the forties and fifties. The New Critics in America were saying that a poem cannot be paraphrased.[7] You cannot take a poem and say what its meaning is in prose terms. You cannot even say what an individual metaphor means in prose terms,[8] because none of those prose descriptions of the metaphor or the poem are ever going to say fully what is expressed in the metaphor or poem itself.

The same is true in the case of visual artworks. That is why I link the third table with a discussion of the arts in that essay: you would never try to explain an artwork by describing what it's made of—for example, saying that Jeff Koons's *Balloon Dog (Red)* (1994–2000) upstairs is simply stainless steel, because there are a lot of things that are stainless steel, so it's not just that. Neither are you going to say that *Balloon Dog (Red)* is how it makes you feel, or what it does to the art market. It does those things, too, but there is a little more to it than that.

Any artwork always challenges the first interpretation anyone makes of it, and, generally speaking, the better an artwork, the more it challenges your interpretation, and the less easily paraphrasable it is. The more inexhaustible it is, so to speak. For me, there is no possible knowledge of objects. You can approach objects obliquely or indirectly (metaphorical language is one of the ways that we do this), and that is what an object is. It's something we have to get at sideways. It's something that we can never replace with anything else. We can never translate it perfectly. Just as you can never translate Shakespeare perfectly into some other language, you can never translate an object perfectly into any language. An object is something more than anything that can be said about it, and more than anything that can be done with it. And this actually cuts against the grain of a lot of contemporary philosophy.

I am going to give another example here since my most recent book was on Latour's politics—it's called *Bruno Latour: Reassembling the Political*.[9] I tried to develop the argument that in his philosophy everything is relational, there is nothing more to a thing than how it acts on other things.[10] I was critical of that for various reasons, despite deeply appreciating Latour's work, and then when Pluto Press contacted me and asked who I would recommend to write a book on Latour's politics, I raised my hand. I wanted to do it myself because I didn't really know what Latour's politics were. Though I had been reading him for years and had written a whole book about him already, I was never really sure what his politics were. He scatters political remarks here and there throughout his writings, but then, at other times, it seems as though he thinks *everything* is political, as if any time two actors

6 Graham Harman, "Undermining, Overmining, and Duomining," in *ADD Metaphysics*, ed. Jenna Sutela (Aalto, Finland: Aalto University Design Research Laboratory, 2013), 40–51.

7 Cleanth Brooks, *The Well Wrought Urn: Studies in the Structure of Poetry* (New York: Harcourt, Brace, and World, 1947). For a critical interpretation of this book, see Graham Harman, "The Well-Wrought Broken Hammer: Object-Oriented Literary Criticism," *New Literary History* 43, no. 2 (Spring 2012): 183–203.

8 Max Black, *Models and Metaphors: Studies in Language and Philosophy* (Ithaca, NY: Cornell University Press, 1962).

9 Graham Harman, *Bruno Latour: Reassembling the Political* (London: Pluto, 2014).

10 Graham Harman, *Prince of Networks: Bruno Latour and Metaphysics* (Melbourne: re.press, 2009).

interact, it's somehow political. So I wanted to figure out what was really going on in his politics. And what I found is that, in his politics, I think he is closer to the truth than in his metaphysics.

Latour's politics start off very heavily on one foot. That foot is the Hobbesian one. Thomas Hobbes turns out to be one of the most important influences on Latour. Hobbes often has a nasty reputation as a political philosopher because he thinks the Leviathan, the sovereign state, has the right to crush resistance.[11] More liberal interpretations of Hobbes are possible: some people call him the founder of liberalism, for the very reason that he wants to prevent all violence within the Leviathan by giving the state a monopoly on violence.[12] In Latour's case, what's important about Hobbes is that he did not allow for any transcendence: nothing was allowed to transcend the polis.

Hobbes, of course, was living during the bloody English Civil War, and he wanted to prevent this from ever happening again. And one of the things that was important to him is to say that there can never be a religious truth that one can appeal to outside of the state, beyond the state. Why not? Because then all kinds of extremists could start appealing directly to a religious truth and using that truth to disobey the state. And Hobbes did not want this, so he wanted religion under state control. He even wanted the state to be responsible for deciding which miracles count as legitimate and which do not. The state was going to rule on each and every miracle, which ones you are forced to believe as a citizen of the state. And you might, in the back of your mind, believe in some other miracle that the state had not sanctioned, but at least you're supposed to outwardly believe in the ones that the state has determined to be real miracles.

Well, that's one problem for Hobbes. He does not want any religious transcendence of the political sphere. Another problem that's less well known is that Hobbes did not want any *scientific* transcendence of the political sphere. He did not want anyone claiming to have scientific truths able to teach them that the government is wrong about this or that. So Hobbes surely would not have supported Galileo, for instance, in his conflict with the Catholic Church.

Steven Shapin and Simon Schaffer have written one of the classics of science and technology studies about the air pump that was invented by Robert Boyle. In fact, there was a conflict between Boyle and Hobbes over this device.[13] Boyle thought that he could actually produce a vacuum inside of a tube with this pump and have a certain number of trustworthy gentleman witnesses testifying to this vacuum that had been created. And this was considered the dawn of the modern scientific article, Boyle's work on the air pump.

Now Hobbes was not only very suspicious of this—because it produced a supposed immaterial thing called a vacuum, which offended Hobbes as a materialist—but because it was also a kind of scientific truth that Boyle was appealing to that could contradict what the state says. And Hobbes actually reported Boyle to the authorities for this. He put his money where his mouth was and reported the great Boyle, saying effectively: "This is dangerous. He is conducting experiments that might destabilize the state."

Well, Hobbes is important for Latour for a similar reason. Latour also does not like any transcendent claims to truth. For him, truth is a matter of putting actors together and creating more and more convincing statements by assembling evidence from inanimate objects, as well as evidence from humans. All these things combine in stronger and stronger networks, and this is what produces truth. Truth does not refer to some objective thing existing outside the mind but is a subspecies of force. Statements are either convincing or unconvincing: this is the early Latour who likes to talk like Hobbes and Machiavelli[14]—he says that Machiavelli was great; there is no difference between might and right.[15]

And, in fact, one of the reviewers of my book proposal when I sent it to Pluto Press made the remark that they were glad I was writing this book, but they didn't think Latour's politics would turn out to be that interesting because it will just turn out to be "might makes right." I can understand that worry about Latour, and it is actually true of his early career. When the young Latour talks about politics, he does have a tendency to say there is no difference between might and right. He tells us that political moralists make a very sorry spectacle because there is no use in being right but failing to achieve victory. For early Latour, it's really a *philosophy of victory*, teaching you how to win by assembling as many black boxes as possible to try to attain victory over your opponents. And

11 Thomas Hobbes, *Leviathan* (Oxford: Oxford University Press, 1996).
12 Leo Strauss, *Natural Right and History* (Chicago: University of Chicago Press, 1953).
13 Steven Shapin and Simon Schaffer, *Leviathan and the Air-Pump: Hobbes, Boyle, and the Experimental Life* (Princeton, NJ: Princeton University Press, 2017).
14 Michel Callon and Bruno Latour, "Unscrewing the Big Leviathan: How Actors Macrostructure Reality and How Sociologists Help Them to Do So," in *Advances in Social Theory and Methodology: Toward an Integration of Micro- and Macro-Sociologies*, ed. Karin Knorr-Cetina and Aaron V. Cicourel (London: Routledge and Kegan Paul, 1981), 11–32.
15 Niccolò Machiavelli, *The Prince*, trans. Peter Bondanella (Oxford: Oxford University Press, 2008).

this is why scientific realists have never liked Latour because he seems to be saying that truth is simply a matter of force or power, that no one can appeal to a truth outside of that power, and so on. That is what the early Latour looks like.

However, something very important happens in *We Have Never Been Modern*, his major book published in French in 1991.[16] He talks there about Shapin and Schaffer's conclusions, and he suddenly seems to realize: Wait a minute, how can we deconstruct truth and not deconstruct power? Is power really as simple as they make it out to be? Shapin and Schaffer do end their book by saying that Hobbes was right because scientific discourse is simply a subspecies of social power discourse: society sets the standards of what counts as good scientific work. And therefore, they think that Hobbes subsumes science underneath his politics. But Latour says that this can't possibly be true; power is just as problematic as truth is. And this leads him off in a different direction, where he begins by saying Hobbes was wrong. Hobbes is not *right* that all truth can be reduced to power. Politics is not just about power. There is also a truth involved in politics; we simply cannot access it. So, Latour starts to sound more and more like Socrates.

You can see this new path of Latour in the late nineties, especially in his book *Politics of Nature*.[17] Whereas before he was a Hobbesian who had no interest at all in any political truth that could challenge what society has said, in *Politics of Nature*, he adds two professions who have no other job than to make just such a challenge. They are the scientists and the moralists. What do scientists and moralists do in *Politics of Nature*? Well, the scientists detect new entities that were not previously recognized by the polis. Climate change would be an obvious example of this. Our governments have not been taking account of this for decades because they didn't know about it, and it was the scientists' job to warn us that this was happening. Or … what was it when I was a kid in the 1970s? Chlorofluorocarbons were destroying the ozone layer. These were things that scientists were supposed to inform the state about, during the middle period of Latour's thinking from 1991 up through the early aughts.

So scientists do that, whereas moralists tell us about social groups that are being marginalized: the Roma in France, or whatever group you can think of that needs to be given more rights. So, the politics of middle Latour is all about detecting things that transcend the state, things that need to be recognized by the state and brought into the tent. And even if they are rejected for now, we might bring them back later. So, for now, we are not really accepting the right of animals not to be killed for meat. Maybe in the future, some state will decide that animals should have the same rights as humans. Who knows? Anything could happen centuries from now. But the point is, these are things that transcend the polis as it is currently constituted.

So where does this leave Latour politically? This leads him, at least in the early twenty-first century, to start paying close attention to Walter Lippmann and John Dewey. Lippmann and Dewey are not often regarded as major political philosophers, but Latour, under the influence of his Dutch student Noortje Marres, started taking these figures very seriously.[18] Lippmann is mostly forgotten today, but in his time in the 1920s and 1930s, he was probably the world's most famous journalist. He met with kings and was the confidant of celebrities. And Lippmann wrote a rather cynical book about American democracy.[19]

American democracy was supposed to be about educating its citizens so that they can rule themselves, and so forth. And we see how well that has worked: not very well. The public is often quite ignorant of important issues; demagogues easily manipulate the American public; and so forth.[20] Lippmann was worried that America was going to turn slowly into a technocracy, and in certain periods of his career, he really saw no other alternative to this because the public cannot possibly stay informed about all the issues.

Dewey read these thoughts from Lippmann, and took them seriously, but drew the exact opposite conclusions.[21] Very interesting conclusions. Dewey said: Yes, this happens, but it's nothing to bemoan, it's just the way things work. Not everybody can stay informed about all issues at all times. Even Lippmann, the most educated journalist of his day, could not possibly have informed opinions on every last political issue. Some of them were very local issues that were of no interest to him. So Latour talks in his new book, *An Inquiry into Modes of Existence*, about object-oriented

16 Bruno Latour, *We Have Never Been Modern*, trans. Catherine Porter (Cambridge, MA: Harvard University Press, 1993).
17 Bruno Latour, *Politics of Nature: How to Bring the Sciences into Democracy*, trans. Catherine Porter (Cambridge, MA: Harvard University Press, 2004).
18 Noortje Marres, "No Issue, No Public: Democratic Deficits after the Displacement of Politics" (PhD diss., University of Amsterdam, 2005).
19 Walter Lippmann, *The Phantom Public* (New Brunswick, NJ: Transaction, 1993).
20 At the time of this lecture, Donald J. Trump was not yet even an announced candidate for president of the United States.
21 John Dewey, *The Public and Its Problems* (University Park, PA: Penn State University Press, 2012).

politics.[22] And he did actually steal that term from me, darn him [*laughter from the audience*] because he heard me introduce this term in 1999, in London.[23] Now he is talking about object-oriented democracy, object-oriented politics. What he means is that every issue or every object defines its own public.

There is not a constant group called "the public" that has to be kept informed about everything. We all duck in and out of the political sphere as issues arise that concern us, or don't concern us, or bore us, or interest us. And this is what democracy is about. It's not about demanding constant self-education and constant personal presence of every political issue, but it means that we dive in where things are of concern to us. And this, for Latour, is what object-oriented democracy is about: it's about the fact that, as concerns the object of politics, we are never going to be entirely clear what it is. All the various stakeholders on an issue gather and have a debate about it, and reach a settlement about it that tries to satisfy all the relevant parties, and then that public disappears and another public emerges for another issue, and so forth.

So this is where Latour was politically for sure, say, ten years ago, in 2005. Now, my sense is that he might be drifting back in the Hobbesian direction over the past few years. The reason for this is that if you read his Gifford Lectures about the environment, about climate change, he seems to be drifting in the direction of Carl Schmitt, who is another one of those reactionary figures often mentioned in the same breath as Hobbes and Machiavelli. Schmitt, of course, thinks the political *proper* happens only when all questions of right and wrong have gone out the window because we've reached a state of exception where the question is existential struggle.[24]

So, let me give you an example from Egypt, and something that is going to happen in Egypt over the next fifteen or twenty years. Forget about Egypt's tensions with Israel; that's not going to be Egypt's political problem. The problem is going to be water. Egypt is a very heavily desert country with a growing population. They are going to have big water problems. And they have a dam (they built a dam in the 1950s, the Aswan High Dam), which dams up the Nile into a big lake, and this is where they get their water. From the 1970s, under Sadat, it was stated in Egyptian foreign policy that they will bomb any dam constructed by another country on the Nile. Their argument defending this is that they have a treaty that they signed—all these countries in Africa signed a treaty in the late 1940s, I think it was, specifying which countries receive which percentage of Nile water, and they were all supposed to stick to this agreement.

Well, in recent years, the sub-Saharan African countries on the Nile have grown to resent this. And one of the reasons they resent it is that this treaty was signed under British colonialism, and so they say: We are absolved from obeying this. This was not the people of sub-Saharan Africa speaking in our own name; this was an arrangement by the British Empire. We don't feel bound by it at all. Then Egypt answers: Yes, but you guys have rain, we don't; the Nile is the only water we have, and a few oases. And the sub-Saharan African countries reply: Yes, but you guys waste a lot of your water; you do not have very efficient irrigation practices, and you need to improve your efficiency with the water you have before you start demanding a higher share of it. And the Egyptians respond: You are also very inefficient in your own irrigation practices, so don't point a finger at us. And this goes on and on.

What's interesting about this issue is that it's very hard to tell who's right if you study it. It's very hard to reach a *moral* conclusion about this water issue in Africa, and it's going to be impossible for anybody to reach a moral solution or moral compromise because, at some point, it's simply going to be a question of life or death for multiple countries. And when things get to that point, we generally have war, where people do not see any alternative other than armed conflict to solving the resource question.

So this is the kind of situation Schmitt, at his best, can illuminate. He would say that you have this state of exception in which you cannot appeal to questions of right or wrong, and it's simply a question of survival. It is interesting that Schmitt, despite being a Nazi, often claims that liberals are worse because they have to define their enemies as morally evil. They have to define their enemies as completely evil, as with Hitler or Saddam Hussein as portrayed in the media of the liberal countries. Whereas Schmitt says, we just have to defeat the enemy, we do not have to annihilate the enemy as something immoral and evil; it's simply a practical matter, we have to save ourselves. Anyway, Schmitt is generally regarded as a sinister figure, but he is often popular on the left as well, because, for them, he is at least being honest about politics being a form of violence. And, of course, what the Left often doesn't

22 Bruno Latour, *An Inquiry into Modes of Existence: An Anthropology of the Moderns*, trans. Catherine Porter (Cambridge, MA: Harvard University Press, 2013).

23 Graham Harman, *Towards Speculative Realism: Essays and Lectures* (Winchester, UK: Zero Books, 2010), chap. 6.

24 Carl Schmitt, *The Concept of the Political*, trans. George Schwab (Chicago: University of Chicago Press, 2007).

like about liberals is what they see as their hypocrisy about the question of violence, and the fact that violence is used to constitute the state.

Now, what has been pushing Latour back to Schmitt is the question of climate change. In his Gifford Lectures, Latour takes a very interesting line that I have called "Green Schmittianism."[25] I've never seen anything quite like it. He is basically saying: We have reached the point where we have to stop debating with climate-change skeptics, and simply declare war on them and beat them. I don't think he means physically killing them, but he does mean simply defeat them in any way possible because there is already enough evidence to convince us that climate change is happening. We are never going to reach total direct scientific certainty, just as Socrates cannot reach direct knowledge. But there comes a point when you have to act. And this is why Schmitt is so important politically for Latour. So he seems to be drifting back into the direction of power politics after his decade-long object-oriented period in which he was talking about political issues as hidden things that we all have to debate about.

So, I have talked a bit about why I think philosophy and the arts are natural allies. Philosophy, since the 1600s, has been trying to mimic the conditions of the natural sciences and deductive geometry. I would agree with Alfred North Whitehead that it's a very bad idea to model philosophy after deductive geometry. Because philosophy is, as Whitehead puts it, a form of descriptive generalization.[26] Philosophy is not about finding some unshakeable first truth and then deducing other truths from it. In philosophy, when it works best, deduction is actually not a very common procedure. As Whitehead also puts it, philosophies are never refuted, they are simply abandoned.[27] A philosophy doesn't die because someone comes up with knock-down arguments against it. Philosophies generally die because they come to seem too narrow, to have too many arbitrary assumptions, or do not seem to describe the world as we know it very well.

An example that Whitehead gives is: What's the problem with Aristotle and Plato? They didn't know about the cell theory of biology. For them, living things were automatically units. There was no issue for them of understanding how living things were made up of multiple units, such as cells and organs. So he thinks this is how Plato and Aristotle became somewhat out of date, not because someone "refuted them." Anyone can come up with twenty arguments against Plato, but Plato is still more interesting than over 99 percent of philosophers working today or at any time.

So, philosophy and the arts go together naturally, I think, because the arts do not really paraphrase objects, but *create* objects. You cannot replace an artwork with any description of it. An artwork is something unified, something that you cannot replace by a prose description. And there are other cases like this besides art. Wine tasting is an example I often use, because Daniel Dennett, who is a fairly reductive American philosopher, makes fun of wine tasting. He talks about a wine taster, maybe fictional, who says: "A flamboyant and velvety pinot, but lacking in stamina."[28] And Dennett basically says: Isn't that pretentious and ridiculous? You should just do a chemical analysis of the wine: that's real wine tasting! OK, fine. You need the chemical analysis. But there's something happening with the human experience of wine that demands this kind of indirect poetic language, to get at the flavor. And yes, that can be pretentious. But pretension is simply the professional risk that we run in the humanities and the arts because we have to describe things using indirect language. We shouldn't be ashamed of this. We should be willing to run the risk of pretension.

You are not going to find a pretentious scientist in most cases. You might find a narrow-minded scientist, a dogmatic scientist, but you are never going to find a pretentious scientist. Why not? Because look at what scientists do for a living: they replace names of objects with prose descriptions of those objects. By way of experiments and other techniques, the name "electron" is gradually replaced with a list of all the true facts about electrons, until maybe you finally have them all, or maybe a few are left mysterious. That's not what you do in the arts. You don't try to replace a Picasso painting gradually with truer and truer descriptions of the painting. That's never going to happen. The art critic, the architecture critic, the food critic, the wine critic, and the philosopher are always going to be moving around the outside of the thing, trying to give descriptions of it indirectly.

Let me move on to philosophy now and talk about my background. I made it sound, in the first step, as though all philosophers and scientists are very anti-object because they were either reducing things downward to particles or they were reducing things upward to their effects. And, in fact, there have been some object-

25 Bruno Latour, *Facing Gaia: Eight Lectures on the New Climatic Regime*, trans. Catherine Porter (Cambridge: Polity, 2017).
26 Alfred North Whitehead, *Process and Reality* (New York: Free Press, 1978), 10.
27 Whitehead, *Process and Reality*, 6.
28 Daniel Dennett, "Quining Qualia," in *Consciousness in Contemporary Science*, ed. Anthony Marcel and Edoardo Bisiach (Oxford: Oxford University Press, 1988).

oriented schools in the history of philosophy, though I don't think any of them have gone far enough. The first school we have to mention will be Aristotle and Gottfried Wilhelm Leibniz, the much later disciple of Aristotle (centuries later).[29]

What characterizes Aristotle? He was the first philosopher in the West to take individual things as being the primary substances the world is made of. So it's not water, it's not atoms, it's horses and plants and things like that. Humans ... These are the primary substances for Aristotle. Leibniz did this as well. The difference being that, for Aristotle, these substances can be destroyed. He didn't believe in the immortality of these substances: horses can be killed, people can die, plants can die. Whereas, for Leibniz, any living thing that dies, its monad would continue to float around in the world. Human souls, in particular, are immortal for Leibniz, as a good Christian.

The problem with this kind of thinking about substances, as I see it, is that they were very focused on natural things. The real object is the natural—so it's plants, animals, individual people that are real for the most part; water, and other things like this, as well. "Natural kinds," as they are sometimes called. Things that occur in nature. Specific familiar types of objects. And this makes it impossible for someone like Aristotle to help us much in contemporary social theory or contemporary art theory, where, usually, we are not dealing with natural things, but with artificial things. We are dealing with machines, we are dealing with international institutions, with political entities.

I am about to challenge myself to write a book on the Dutch East India Company[30] because it's one of Leibniz's favorite examples of a ridiculous object that can't possibly be a real object.[31] Because it has many different people, many different ships, many different offices, and the exact boundaries of the Dutch East India Company and its power change over time. But I am going to argue the opposite: that it is a real thing that endures for a certain period of time. It's not immortal, but it can add and subtract elements and still remain the same company, within certain limits.

There is also Immanuel Kant. And since philosophy moves so slowly, Kant is still our living grandfather. He published *Critique of Pure Reason* in 1781, but for the most part, we are all still working in Kant's shadow because of how slowly philosophy moves.[32] For Kant, of course, a big part of his philosophy is that there are the things-in-themselves that lie beyond the human mind. We can think about them, but we can never know them. Why not? Because we are trapped in space and time, because we know humans experience everything in space and time. This does not prove that there *really* is space and time outside the human mind. Also, there are twelve categories of the understanding for Kant, things like cause and effect. We don't really know if things happen according to cause and effect outside the mind because we can never get outside it. So Kant does talk about objects, and he talks—as I do—about objects as impenetrable to any direct form of knowledge, any form of paraphrase.

The problem, for me, with Kant is that he restricts this to being simply a human problem. That we poor humans have this major difficulty that we cannot reach the things-in-themselves. Poor us! We are tragic, finite creatures! But what about objects interacting with each other? Objects interacting with each other *also* do not make contact with the full totality of each other. When fire burns cotton, the fire does not make contact with all the properties of the cotton. The fire is relatively stupid, just as humans are. When humans hold cotton balls in our hands, we are not making contact with all the features of the cotton ball. But when fire burns the cotton ball … well, the fire might not be alive as we are, and it might not be conscious as we are, but the fire will still only be touching certain features of the cotton, the ones that are relevant to its own existence.

So objects distort and translate each other as well. It's not just humans that do this. The difference between humans and fire is another question. It's not a *fundamental* ontological question. Ontologically speaking, at the most basic level, every object distorts or translates every other object it encounters. This is a general problem throughout all of philosophy. And this idea actually comes out of Islamic philosophy, and from a fairly conservative brand of it. From early on in Islam, we have the so-called Ash'arites in Basra, in what is now southern Iraq.[33] All monotheist philosophers, of course, had said that God is the only *creator*. But the

29 Gottfried Wilhelm Leibniz, *Philosophical Essays*, trans. Roger Ariew and Daniel Garber (Indianapolis, IN: Hackett, 1989).

30 The book was eventually published as Graham Harman, *Immaterialism: Objects and Social Theory* (Cambridge: Polity, 2016).

31 Leibniz, *Philosophical Essays*, 89.

32 Immanuel Kant, *Critique of Pure Reason*, trans. Norman Kemp Smith (New York: St. Martin's Press, 1965).

33 Majid Fakhry, *A History of Islamic Philosophy* (New York: Columbia University Press, 2004), 215–33; Majid Fakhry, *Islamic Occasionalism: And Its Critique by Averroes and Aquinas* (New York: Routledge, 2008); Dominik Perler and Ulrich Rudolph, *Occasionalismus: Theorien der Kausalität im arabisch-islamischen und im europäischen Denken* (Göttingen: Vandenhoeck & Ruprecht, 2000).

Ash'arites took it a step further by saying that God is the only causal agent at all, and it's blasphemous to say otherwise. There is a certain passage in the Qur'an about the Battle of Badr, where, against all odds, the Muslims defeated the infidels. And at 8:17 we read, concerning the Prophet's defeat of the enemy: "And you did not kill them, but it was Allah who killed them. And you threw not, [O Muhammad], when you threw, but it was Allah who threw that He might test the believers with a good test. Indeed, Allah is Hearing and Knowing."[34]

Of course, the obvious way to interpret this passage is that this battle was miraculous. It was divine intervention. Allah intervened in this particular battle so that the Muslims would survive. The Ash'arites, however, took it in a much broader sense to mean that not just the stones being thrown at that particular battle require divine intervention, but even me picking up the water glass right now [*picking up a water glass*]. I think I am picking up the water glass, but in fact, it is Allah who is picking up the water glass. God intervenes in every causal interaction in the cosmos. Well, this took a long time to pass into Europe. And it passed into Europe through a famous Stockholm resident, René Descartes, the unfortunate Frenchman who died here, and was once buried here, I was told, before his bones were relocated to Paris.

For Descartes, of course, the two finite substances are mind and body. And since those are different substances, it's hard to know how they can communicate, and so God is the infinite substance brought in to bridge the gap.[35] His intellectual heir, Nicolas Malebranche, pushed this even further to object-object interactions, in a sort of throwback to the era of Islamic occasionalism.[36] God is intervening in those as well. It's not just the mind-body interaction, but with any two objects interacting, God has to come in. And then, of course, there are other philosophers in the seventeenth century, such as Leibniz, Spinoza, and Berkeley—all of them bringing in God in some way in order to explain causal relation between different things.

Now, this may sound quaint to us today. It may sound as if this was what philosophers used to think back when they were religious, and isn't it great that we got rid of religion now and are more secular? Except that the same idea still exists in Western philosophy to this very day. It's simply not God anymore: it's the human mind that monopolizes causation. Among those philosophers who are still contemporary for us, we find Hume and Kant. And what do Hume and Kant tell us about cause and effect? Hume tells us that cause and effect is simply a habit.[37] Every time somebody puts their hand in a fire, it seems to hurt. So, therefore, there is a very high probability that the fire is causing the hurt, even though we can't prove it. It's the same idea as the Occasionalists, that the human mind (rather than God) must be on the scene every time a supposed causal event occurs. The human mind is what forms all the habits, and leads us to think there is cause and effect. Kant makes it even easier to prove this point because he explicitly thinks that cause and effect is a category of our understanding. So again, it's the human mind that makes cause and effect happen, nothing in the outside world.

And an interesting thing happened even in the twentieth century on this question of occasionalism, as we call it in philosophy—occasionalism being the idea that God is intervening everywhere. I told you that Hume and Kant replaced God with the human mind—the human mind was always there as the glue for any causal relation. But in the 1920s, Whitehead brought back God as the universal causal glue, which is a very daring and even crazy move to make at such a late date. It sounds like a seventeenth-century sort of idea rather than a twentieth-century one.

Whitehead's idea is that I see light from that colored sweater there [*pointing at a person in the audience*], and, actually, that sweater is all the colors of the rainbow, and God can see that when he looks at this sweater. But I, being a stupid human, objectify it into just one color. I am passing through God, through the "eternal object" of that color, and objectifying the shirt in terms of that color. Then, there is Latour, who, in fact, is probably even more religious than Whitehead was. Latour is a very serious practicing Catholic, but he doesn't usually bring God into his philosophical arguments the way Whitehead does. Latour tries to give a more secular version of occasionalism, with the example of Frédéric Joliot-Curie and the atomic bomb.[38]

Joliot-Curie was the son-in-law of Marie and Pierre Curie. He and his wife Irène, the Curies' daughter, both later won Nobel Prizes of their own. But for Latour's story, the important thing is that Joliot-Curie was the first person in France to link politics with neutrons. James Chadwick in England discovered the neutron,

34 Qur'an, Sahih International translation.
35 René Descartes, *Meditations on First Philosophy*, trans. Donald Cress (Indianapolis, IN: Hackett, 1993).
36 Nicolas Malebranche, *Dialogues on Metaphysics and on Religion*, trans. David Scott (Cambridge: Cambridge University Press, 1997).
37 David Hume, *A Treatise of Human Nature* (Oxford: Oxford University Press, 1978).
38 Latour, *Pandora's Hope*, chap. 3.

and, of course, when it was first discovered, it seemed completely apolitical. Who could think that there is any political value in the neutron? No one! But then, just a few years later, it was determined that neutrons were extremely valuable in splitting the atom. So neutrons became a charged political object, and Joliot-Curie tried, unsuccessfully, to persuade the French Ministry of Defense to invest heavily in an atomic bomb project. They weren't able to make much progress on it before they were knocked out of the war. But Latour takes this as a paradigm case of what causation is all about. He says that no two things can relate unless there is a third term in between that relates them, no matter what example you take.

There is a problem with this, however. If Joliot-Curie is what bridges politics and neutrons and makes them touch, how can Joliot-Curie touch politics, and how can he touch neutrons? The same problem occurs there. And you could say: OK, Joliot-Curie touches neutrons through a scientific instrument. But how does he touch the scientific instrument? Through his eyeball. And how does Joliot-Curie touch his eyeball? Through his nervous system. How does Joliot-Curie touch his nervous system? Through his brain. You can keep going backward, regressing further and further, and you are going to push the problem further and further back, always finding the same problem.

Latour's answer to this is a disappointing, pragmatic answer, which is that you simply stop when it gets boring [*laughter from the audience*]. Now, this may work for the purposes of sociological analysis, but it doesn't work for the purposes of philosophy, metaphysics. You have to be able to explain, for the purposes of metaphysics, how any two things can touch at all. The reason Latour cannot ever explain this, I hold, is because he only has one kind of object. He has a completely flat ontology: all objects are actors, they come only in one kind. So, anytime you have two actors together, there has to be a third one in between the first two, and it goes on in an infinite regress and nothing can ever touch.

So the only possible solution is to have two different kinds of objects. Otherwise, we get something like Zeno's paradoxes. How do you get outside of this auditorium? You can't. Because first, I have to go halfway to the door. And once I am there, I have to go half the distance between there and the door. And once I am there, I again have to go half the distance, and so we are going to get closer and closer to the door, but never outside the auditorium. This can't explain how anything interacts, if that's how things work.

I am going to tell you now why I think there are exactly two kinds of objects, just as there are exactly two poles of magnets, north and south. This is how you make a chain of magnets: you don't try to touch north and north together, because they repel each other. But if you have two kinds of objects, you can connect an infinite number of objects in sequence, and that is what I think is needed.

Here, I need to talk about phenomenology, and then I'll end with some thoughts about the arts—the transition is easier than it sounds [*laughter from the audience*]. Let's talk about Edmund Husserl and Martin Heidegger, who can be grouped generally under the heading of phenomenology. This is my favorite object-oriented brand of philosophy. Most people don't usually see it as object-oriented, but I think that's the key to both of these thinkers. Let's start briefly with Husserl in an unfair way, and we'll come back to him in a fair way later.

Husserl, of course, is the founder of phenomenology. It was founded in his *Logical Investigations* in 1900 and 1901, after twelve years of suffering during which Husserl sometimes doubted whether he had any philosophical ability at all. It became a groundbreaking work. And one of the key principles of phenomenology is that we should simply describe things as they appear to us, as a first step. Don't invent theories about unseen things. What Husserl is doing here is trying to prevent the sciences from taking over philosophy, as they seemed to be doing in the late 1800s. They are doing it again now, with neurophilosophy trying to replace us with neuroscience (some of them, at least).[39] Husserl said that the problem with scientific theories is not that they are false. No, they are probably true. Instead, the problem with scientific theories is that they are *mediated*. They are not directly what we see.

So, when you hear a door slam, you don't immediately jump ahead to the physiological theory of how you are hearing that sound. I don't say too quickly that it's because sound waves are moving through the air, vibrating my eardrum, going up my nervous system, creating a chemical pattern in my brain, and so forth. This is probably true, but it's not the first thing we experience. The first thing we experience is simply the slamming of the door. Even if I am not looking at the door, I say "that's a door slamming," and I turn around and, yes, it's a door slamming. There are all kinds of psychological subtleties in our experience of the door slamming that Husserl invites us to describe in painstaking detail,

39 See Wolf Singer's remark in Thomas Metzinger, *The Ego Tunnel: The Science of the Mind and the Myth of the Self* (New York: Basic Books, 2010), 71.

until we finally reach the essence of what that sound really has as its core, that makes it the sound of a door slamming rather than some other sound. In how many different ways could we vary it without changing the fact that it's the sound of a door slamming?

More about Husserl in a bit. But Heidegger's criticism of him is as follows: Heidegger was, of course, Husserl's star student. But as early as his Freiburg Lecture Course in 1919, when he was twenty-nine years old, Heidegger argued that this is not the primary way we encounter things.[40] The primary way we encounter things is by taking them for granted, not having them consciously in mind. So, take the floor in this room, the most important thing in this space. If the floor were to disappear, we would all fall and become dead or seriously injured. But you weren't thinking about the floor, most likely, until I mentioned it. You weren't thinking about the oxygen in the room until I mentioned it just now. But we all need it here to survive. There is the entire vast background of things that we need, such as political stability in the streets of Stockholm. If we were in Egypt's Tahrir Square right now, we would not be able to sit here comfortably listening to a lecture. There are all these background things we take for granted and, as Heidegger argues, we normally notice these things only when they malfunction in some way. You don't usually think of your bodily organs until they start having a pain or medical complication, and you don't normally think of solid ground until there is an earthquake, and so forth.

So, for Heidegger, the deeper level is this hidden layer, this hidden background that only erupts occasionally, usually in cases of malfunction. And Heidegger has a tendency to treat this entire background region as one unified being, one unified lump. I think that was his mistake. Namely, his mistake was in not accounting sufficiently for the fact that each object has its own background. Someone who does this very well, however, is Marshall McLuhan, of all people, the great Canadian media theorist, who says that every medium has a background, and the background is what is most important about it.[41] So, when it comes to television, whether a television show is good or bad is not especially important to McLuhan. Instead, the important thing is that you are watching television rather than listening to the radio, and that has certain consequences for how your brain organizes the world. Television is what he calls a cold medium, not a hot medium, so it's more hypnotic. And there are all these other features of the background medium.

McLuhan and Heidegger, then, are theorists of the background. They think the foreground is superficial. You don't need to care so much about how things appear. In this way, Heidegger is trying to turn phenomenology upside-down, and he gets what I would call "real objects." Real objects are the ones that withdraw, that never become visible even when they break. From using a hammer when it breaks, I become conscious of the hammer, but there is still more depth in that hammer that I cannot exhaust. The hammer is always deeper than any interaction we have with it. It's not just that "praxis is deeper than theory," but that the hammer, as an object, is deeper than any human interaction with it whatsoever, and ultimately deeper than the interaction between any two objects, whether they are human or not. With two asteroids colliding in distant space, the same thing happens. They are not fully grasping each other. There is more depth in each of those asteroids than either of the asteroids can react to.

All right, so that's Heidegger. But now we need to go back to Husserl because we were unfair to him a few minutes ago. What really is the chief insight of Husserl? I would say that it's the following, and you are not going to find this same answer anywhere in the Husserl scholarship: For me, it's that Husserl reversed British empiricism. One of the primary lessons of that school, in figures such as Locke and Hume, is that there isn't really an object.[42] There is no such thing as an object, there are just "bundles of qualities." So you think you are holding an apple in your hand, but actually, you are just holding a bundle of qualities. You are holding red, brown, juicy, hard, sweet, cold, and all these qualities appear together so often in your hands that you start giving them all a collective nickname. I call this bundle "apple," even though I never do see an apple, I just see these qualities. That is what empiricism thinks about objects. They aren't really there. There is just a loose nickname for a bunch of qualities that appear together over and over again, repeatedly.

In a way, the key insight of phenomenology is simply to reverse that idea and say that the object comes first, the qualities come second. And so, Husserl gives some good examples of this in his *Logical Investigations*.[43] He says, for example, you see your friend Hans walking down the street. Well, I would say: There is my

40 Martin Heidegger, *Towards the Definition of Philosophy*, trans. Ted Sadler (London: Continuum, 2008).

41 Marshall McLuhan, *Understanding Media: The Extensions of Man* (Cambridge, MA: MIT Press, 1994).

42 John Locke, *An Essay Concerning Human Understanding*, vol. 2 (New York: Dover, 1959); Hume, *A Treatise of Human Nature*.

43 Edmund Husserl, *Logical Investigations*, vols. 1–2, trans. J. N. Findlay (London: Routledge and Kegan Paul, 1970).

friend Hans. He looks a little more depressed today; he is wearing different clothes; he had a haircut since I saw him yesterday. But you're not going to say: This visual image that I see approaching me is 97.3 percent similar to the person yesterday I called my friend Hans [*laughter from the audience*], and therefore, I will arbitrarily say that the family resemblances are such that ... That simply never happens. That's a complete fabrication on the part of empiricism. That's not how it works. What happens is you say: I see my friend Hans; his qualities are a bit different. Now I am walking from behind and seeing him from behind. It's still Hans. I am just seeing another side of him. So the object comes first for phenomenology, not the qualities—the qualities are subservient to the object.

Maurice Merleau-Ponty, being the most beautiful writer of all these people, often gives the best examples. I think he says somewhere that the black of an ink pen and the black of an executioner's hood are not the same black even if the wavelength of light is exactly the same. Because the object in question infects the color with its own atmosphere, so you are going to be scared by the black of an executioner's hood, and you are not going to be scared of the black of an ink pen, even if it's exactly the same black in optical terms. Because the object comes first. This is an important discovery of Husserl that Heidegger and others completely ignore. And that's the idea that, even though Husserl is an idealist, even though Husserl thinks there is no such thing as a world of things-in-themselves outside all possible human perception, he still retains a concept of objects in tension with their qualities. Objects are in tension with qualities because you can change your clothing, you can change your appearance, and I would still recognize you, within certain ill-defined limits, as the same person.

So there is one tension here between objects and qualities, and whereas most philosophies exist in order to collapse distinctions and break them down, object-oriented philosophy is about driving wedges between those distinctions and widening them. And, for us, there are four basic distinctions. Because you have real objects, the kind that Heidegger talks about that always hide, those real objects need real qualities—because if all objects had the same qualities, they'd all be the same. So, for objects to be different, each one must have its own real qualities that are hidden from us. We can never paraphrase them. But then, on the level that I call the sensual, there are also objects and qualities in tension with each other. So there are actually four tensions involved. And, for me, these are the basic facts of philosophy, these four tensions.

And if you look at them closely, you end up with what I call time, space, essence, and eidos in my book *The Quadruple Object*.[44] Again: time, space, essence, and eidos.

I think time and space can be explained in terms of tensions between objects and their qualities. And, usually, time and space are talked about together as peerless dimensions of the universe, but I think essence and eidos—which are different kinds of tension between objects and their qualities—also belong in the same breath. So, really, time and space should be spoken of more phenomenally in terms of tension between objects and their own qualities. And the one that's of interest to us here is the tension between hidden real objects and their visible qualities, because I think this is the one that is relevant to the arts. And, here, I am borrowing from Heidegger's essay "The Origin of the Work of Art," because Heidegger talks about artworks being a strife between earth and world.[45] In that essay, the earth is what withdraws and hides, and the world is what's visible. And there is the tension. The artwork is visible, but it's also not visible. What it makes present is never entirely there, which is a way of saying what I said earlier: that artworks are not paraphrasable. You cannot translate artworks into presence in any way. So I would agree with Heidegger on his basic idea, except that I think his "earth" is, again, too unified. It's too much a single background that all things share, whereas I think that each object has its own background.

Now, here's the transition to art, because this flaw in Heidegger's model of the background is quite similar to Clement Greenberg's problem when he talks about the flat background canvas in painting. I know that Greenberg maybe isn't fully back in fashion yet. He was the only person whose name brought hisses from the crowd in Berlin when I spoke there three years ago at the Transmediale festival.[46] Obviously, he's very unpopular in those circles. But Greenberg, of course, exerted lots of influence in the 1940s, 1950s, and up to the early 1960s: the power to make and break careers, the power to dub Jackson Pollock the great new artist.

On the one hand, the object-oriented philosophy I have talked about seems to be in some agreement with Greenberg, because object-oriented philosophy also talks about the autonomy

44 Graham Harman, *The Quadruple Object* (Winchester, UK: Zero Books, 2011).
45 Martin Heidegger, "The Origin of the Work of Art," in *Off the Beaten Track*, ed. and trans. Julian Young and Kenneth Haynes (Cambridge: Cambridge University Press, 2002).
46 Graham Harman, *Bells and Whistles: More Speculative Realism* (Winchester, UK: Zero Books, 2013), chap. 8.

of objects. And Greenberg talks about the autonomy of artworks from their biographical and sociopolitical surroundings. There is a certain self-containedness or autonomy to artworks. However, I think he draws the wrong conclusions from this, and I will give a few examples. We know how harsh Greenberg could be. He, of course, has no interest in either Dada or Surrealism. He thinks he dislikes them for the same reason, but I would say they are opposites according to the terms Greenberg sets up himself. Though Greenberg is famous for attacking kitsch in his first published essay, I think his real strategic enemy is academic art, as he calls it.[47]

What is academic art? There are a lot of ways to define this. We all know what late-nineteenth-century French academic painting looks like. And we can see why Greenberg wouldn't like that, but he defines academic art toward the end of his career in a way that would please McLuhan a great deal. Namely, Greenberg says, in a late lecture in Australia, that academic art is art that is unaware of its medium.[48] So, one good example of academic art would be art that simply continues to paint three-dimensional objects arranged in three-dimensional space as if we're looking out a window—and here is mainstream painting as we have had it since the Italian Renaissance.

He thinks of this as academic art, and he considers Salvador Dalí to be simply a regressive example of it.[49] Because, even though Dalí paints all these crazy figures and objects in his paintings, he's still just trying to paint a three-dimensional likeness of something you might see when looking out a window. Now, Greenberg admits that Dalí *needs* to do this. He needs to retain the medium as it was, in academic painting, in order to draw our attention to the strange *content*, such as tall flaming giraffes and Wilhelm Tell with the crutch under his giant buttock, as you can see upstairs here.[50] So Greenberg doesn't like Dalí, but at least he admits that Dalí had to do this in order to draw our attention repeatedly to the variations in the content instead of the medium.

And you can do a thought experiment. You can try to imagine a Dalí painting done in the style of Analytical Cubism. It's impossible to make that work, I think. It would simply be too intellectually "busy." To give an example, I love the Dalí painting *The Ghost of Vermeer van Delft Which Can Be Used as a Table* (1934), where Vermeer appears as a ghost and has a very long table with a tray of drinks on it supported on top of his leg. It's a very amusing one. But try to imagine painting this subject in the manner of Picasso and Braque during their high Analytic Cubist period. It would simply be too confusing.

Cubist paintings need simple, banal objects. They need violins and candlesticks because the formal variations are already such a demand on the intellect that you need simple objects to be depicted. And vice versa with Dalí's images: you need a very traditional medium depicting them so that the objects themselves aren't too confusing and hard to detect. You need to be able to see that there really is a flaming giraffe, there really is the ghost of Vermeer, and so forth. Nonetheless, though I can see why Greenberg calls Dalí an academic artist, I cannot so easily see why he calls Duchamp an academic artist. Because if there is anyone who did not "take his medium for granted," it was probably Duchamp. The medium of art has always been challenged in his work, in the readymades and elsewhere. So, though Surrealism and Dada are always lumped together as a package—and you can see why, because they both have a similar sense of humor, and, historically, a lot of people belonged to both movements simultaneously—there's a sense in which Surrealism and Dada are performing opposite thought experiments. One of them retains the old medium and varies the content (Surrealism) while the other (Dada) is doing the reverse.

That's one example of Greenberg's judgments. Another one, which is even crueler, is his obituary essay for Kandinsky, which is probably the cruelest thing Greenberg ever wrote, just a few weeks after Kandinsky's death. He doesn't call Kandinsky an academic artist; he calls him a provincial artist.[51] Now, what's a provincial artist? Well, we know about one kind of provincial artist: someone who lives in a small village, is unaware of advanced art, and simply paints on Sundays as a hobby or as a local painter. This is the usual kind of provincial artist we think of. But Greenberg says there's another kind. This other kind is the artist who is truly right in the thick of things, a colleague of the most advanced artists, but who somehow misunderstands what's going on.

As Greenberg sees it, this is Kandinsky: he misunderstood Cubism. How so? Well, for Greenberg, what Cubism is really about is the flatness of the background medium. Cubism is fully aware that it's not presenting the illusion of three-dimensional space, but it's somehow winking at us and showing us that it knows the canvas

47 Clement Greenberg, *The Collected Essays and Criticism, Volume 1: Perceptions and Judgments, 1939–1944* (Chicago: University of Chicago Press, 1986), 5–22.
48 Clement Greenberg, *Late Writings*, ed. Robert C. Morgan (Minneapolis: University of Minnesota Press, 2003), 28.
49 Greenberg, *Collected Essays and Criticism, Volume 1*, 9.
50 Referring to Dalí's painting *The Enigma of Wilhelm Tell* (1933).
51 Clement Greenberg, *The Collected Essays and Criticism, Volume 2: Arrogant Purpose, 1945–1949* (Chicago: University of Chicago Press, 1988), 3–5.

is flat, by flattening everything out on the same surface and simply depicting planes that show us what the object is. But he thinks Kandinsky misunderstood Cubism to be about *abstraction*, and the result is that, in Greenberg's opinion, Kandinsky has a whole bunch of abstract shapes floating in academic three-dimensional space. He calls it an "academic reminiscence." You get all these triangles and circles and squiggly lines and musical notations floating in a sort of void. And he says this is actually a throwback to nineteenth-century academic painting. He ends up saying that this is a horrible example for younger artists and that Kandinsky may have been a great painter for a few years, earlier on in his career, but it has been a disaster at the end. So very, very harsh.

My main problem with Greenberg, however, is not the usual problem people have with him. The usual problem people have is that he's artificially cutting off artworks from their surroundings, whether these be political or otherwise. Now, I'm all in favor of his notion of the importance of the background, but I don't see why it should be unified and unarticulated. This is where I see the real problem with Greenberg. I don't think the background should be one lump for him, the way it is for Heidegger. Because then the background doesn't really perform any function; it's just a hidden unified lump behind everything else that conditions all of the surface's appearances, so that all the individual elements of a painting simply become surfaces. There's no depth to them at all. Yet it seems to me that the individual elements of an artwork each have their own depth, and so the artwork is less unified, as I see it, than Greenberg or even Heidegger would think.

The artwork actually consists of *numerous* elements that are part of the work: each with its own background, each with its own depth. And I think you can see this easily just by looking at how people create artworks: they are adding and subtracting things up to the last minute. There is not some magical moment when finally it all comes together as a unit so that we can stop. There are individual components to it—and I learned this lesson also from looking at the graffiti in Tahrir Square in Cairo. I imagine that Greenberg would have hated this art: he would have said that it's unaware of the flatness of the masonry background on which it is painted and that it's academic. He would probably not like this art, but I find it quite haunting.

What you find in this graffiti art at Tahrir Square is a whole bunch of discrete objects floating in a kind of abstract space. It's a mixture of Pharaonic objects, images of Egyptian football players, Arabic words, hieroglyphics. All of these things are mixed together and floating in a kind of nonorganized space. There is something very powerful about this. I think it's because each of the elements of the graffiti has its own depth, and these elements are always changing. People spray-paint over it and put up new stuff all the time. So while I am generally in favor of the notion that artworks have a background, that they do not simply consist in their effect on their environments or in their political message, or these sorts of things, there are still many more backgrounds to each artwork than Greenberg or Heidegger would allow.

Now, let me mention briefly before closing the different problems that I have with Michael Fried, who, of course, is often considered the intellectual heir of Greenberg. If you look at Fried's famous work on the Minimalists from 1967, "Art and Objecthood," he makes two complaints about the Minimalists that I do not think go together.[52] I actually think they contradict each other, though he treats them as one and the same. The first problem he has with the Minimalists, he says, is that they are literalists. They are simply putting literal objects in our path and expecting us to consider them as artworks, and for Fried, this is impossible because, for him, as for Greenberg, the artwork has a certain autonomy. It has a depth to it that is not something literally present in the environment, but something that cannot be exhausted or exploited. And I'm willing to go along with that, of course.

But I'm not willing to go along with the second step, which is where Fried says that Minimalist works are also *theatrical*. His reason for saying this is that since they have no internal aesthetic quality and are simply everyday objects lying in our path, their only possible effect as artworks would be the rhetorical or theatrical effect they have on us. I don't see a problem with that, and I think the problem here is that Fried is conflating two aspects of human involvement in artworks. Namely, I would distinguish between humans as observers and humans as ingredients, and not just of artworks, but of other things as well.

As a first example, let's talk about society. Manuel DeLanda published his book *A New Philosophy of Society* in 2006. What DeLanda says at the beginning of that book is, basically, I am trying to talk about society as it is in itself apart from humans.[53] And people say: That's impossible, humans are part of society, how can we talk about human society as something apart from humans? And DeLanda notes that, obviously, human beings are part of human

52 Michael Fried, "Art and Objecthood," in *Art and Objecthood: Essays and Reviews* (Chicago: University of Chicago Press, 1998), 148–72.
53 DeLanda, *A New Philosophy of Society*, 1.

society. If all human beings died, there wouldn't be a human society. Yet, it does not follow from this that human society consists of nothing more than what humans think it is. Society has a real force to it. Sociologists don't know what society is: they keep improving sociology, trying to get closer to the reality of what society is. So, we conclude that humans are an ingredient in human society, yet humans are not transparent observers of human society because we cannot be transparent observers of anything. Objects are always deeper than any access we can have to them, and that includes objects that we ourselves help create.

So I would draw a distinction—and here is a new bit of clever terminology I've come up with—between the anthropocentric and the Anthropocene. Look at climate change. What does climate change tell us? It tells us now that the climate is Anthropocene. We are in the Anthropocene because humans have helped create the climate as it is now. Humans are a major factor in the climate now, unlike before. It does not follow that the climate is anthropocentric: quite the contrary. An anthropocentric climate would be one in which the climate is whatever we think it is. Of course it's not. The climate could kill us all. It's Anthropocene, not anthropocentric. Humans cannot understand the climate down to its very depths, even though humans are now an inescapable ingredient of it.

The same goes for human society. There is no sociologist who can tell you exactly how society works, and there will never be one because society is very complicated, very deep and dark. There will be a continuing series of half-failed efforts to try to understand society, even though humans are an ingredient in it. And I would say the same for the arts. And the reason this came to mind is because people often misunderstand what speculative realism's relation to the arts is about. People come to me, and they say, roughly: We know you are against the human privilege in philosophy over the past four hundred years, so you must also be against the human privilege in the arts. So what would an art without humans look like? And, apparently, they try to imagine artworks that humans can't see or that humans won't know about. But I don't see that this is necessary. In fact, I think humans are a necessary ingredient of every artwork. Yet, it does not follow from this that an artwork is simply its effect on humans; however it may affect the politics of the day or however it affects an observer. No, but we are still ingredients of the artwork. You need a human there for the artwork to be an artwork. For this reason, I think you *need* theater.

And this is also a reason—I'll close with one last thought—that we can retrieve the *classical* sense of mimesis, which is way out of fashion, right? Because mimesis, or imitation, is considered a very old-fashioned idea of what art is about: that you're copying things that are in the real world. But there's a different way to look at mimesis, which is not that you are producing copies of things in the world but that *you yourself* become the copy, which is the mimesis that we know from method acting.[54] You are a rock [*wraps his arms around his body*]; what's your motivation? [*Laughter from the audience.*] This, perhaps, is the ultimate form of mimesis in the arts: that you have to become the thing, the participant is needed as an ingredient in the artwork.[55]

And this, incidentally, is why I'm not quite as far away from Nicolas Bourriaud as some people think. Because Bourriaud writes in *Relational Aesthetics* about how the art of our day that's working well is art that forges encounters between people.[56] They cook packets of noodle soup together in a gallery, and, therefore, they are no longer alienated from each other. And I told a magazine that I was going to write about Bourriaud, and they were worried. They were worried that I was going to trash him completely. They were saying: Oh, but be careful, he was very nice to you in the Taipei Biennial catalogue, so don't be too harsh on him. But actually, I ended up praising Bourriaud in the article to some extent, because what he runs across that's important in his idea of relational aesthetics is that the human *does* play some role in the work.[57] The human is an ingredient of the work, and that's the way in which I depart from formalism. I'll leave it there. I've talked for too long. I await your questions in the gallery later. Thank you!

54 Graham Harman, "A New Sense of Mimesis," in *Aesthetics Equals Politics: New Discourses across Art, Architecture, and Philosophy*, ed. Mark Foster Gage (Cambridge, MA: MIT Press, 2019), 49–63.
55 Konstantin Stanislavski, *An Actor's Work*, trans. Jean Benedetti (London: Routledge, 2010).
56 Nicolas Bourriaud, *Relational Aesthetics* (Dijon: Les presses du réel, 1998).
57 Graham Harman, "Art without Relations," *ArtReview*, no. 66 (September 2014): 144–47.

Thirteen Questions about the Object to Graham Harman

by Daniel Birnbaum
Marcia Cavalcante
Micael Dahlen
Pierre Guillet de Monthoux
Jenny Lantz
Isak Nilson
Sigrid Sandström
Ebba Sjögren
Emma Stenström
Lars Strannegård
Sven-Olov Wallenstein
Jo Widoff
and Erik Wikberg

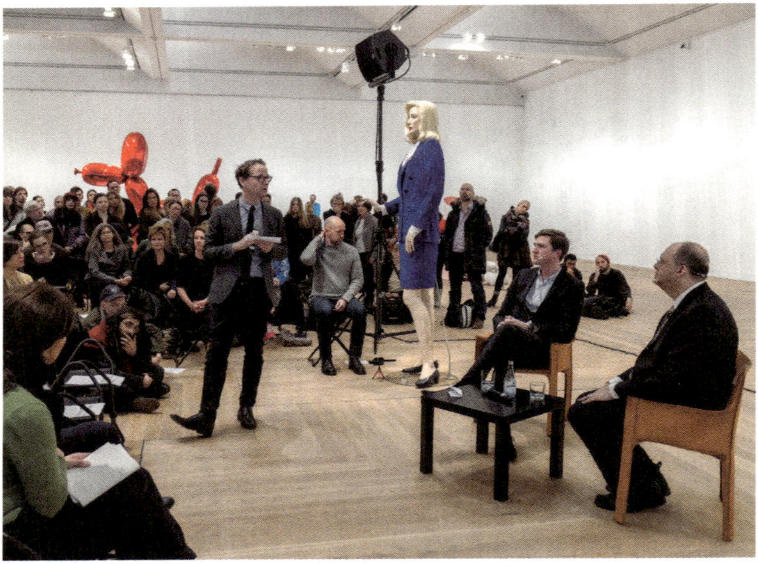

Lars Strannegård posing his question about objects in a digital world to Graham Harman.

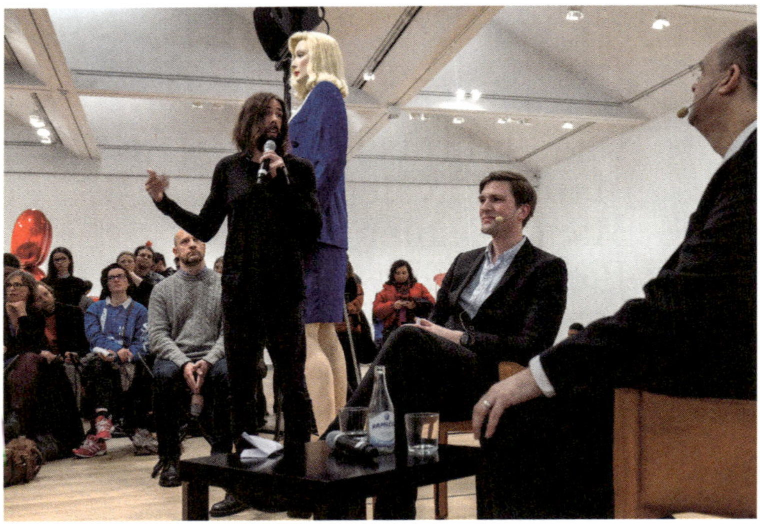

Micael Dahlen asking his question about time, space, and what an object is not.

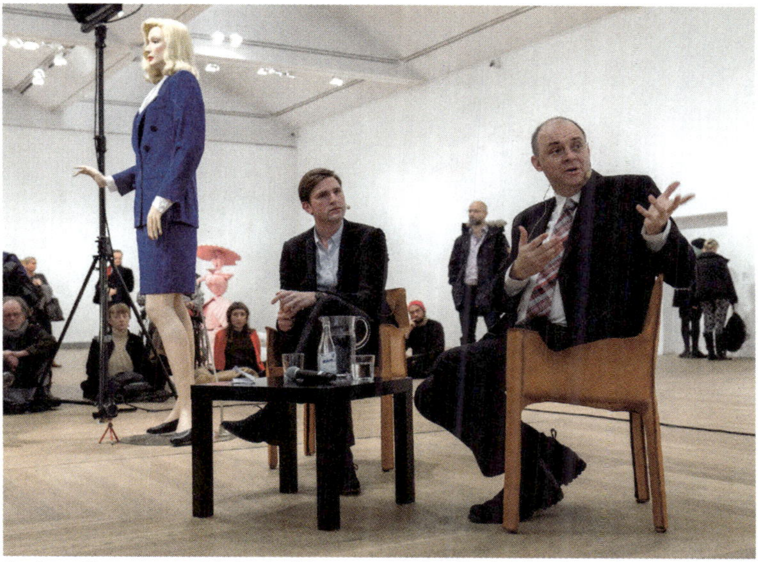

Graham Harman, next to Isak Nilson, answering Daniel Birnbaum's question about whether objects can be traumatized.

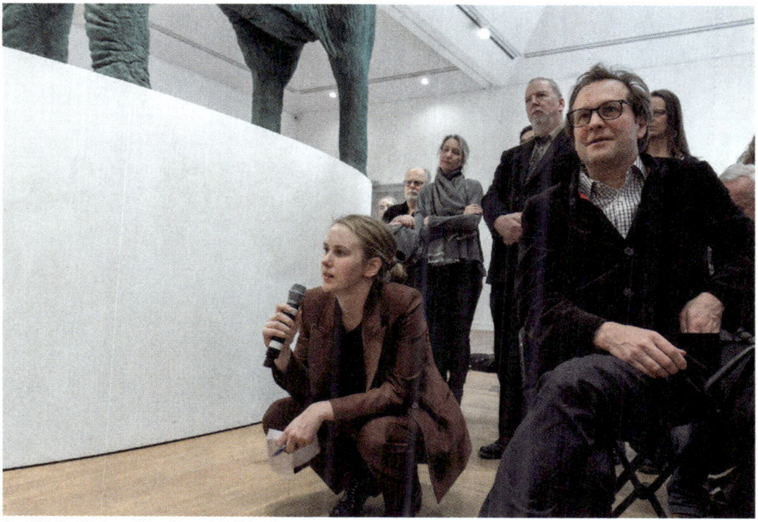

Jo Widoff, beside Daniel Birnbaum,
posing her question about the art part of art objects.

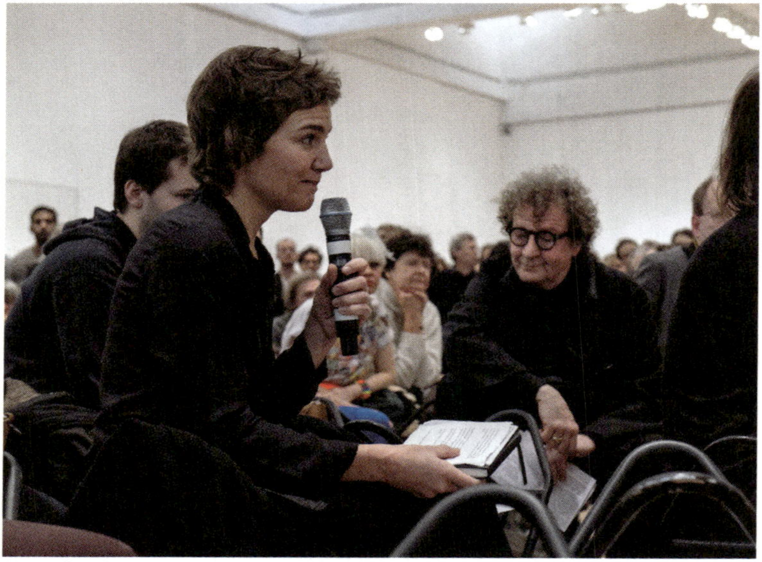

Sigrid Sandström, beside Pierre Guillet de Monthoux, posing her question about object interactions.

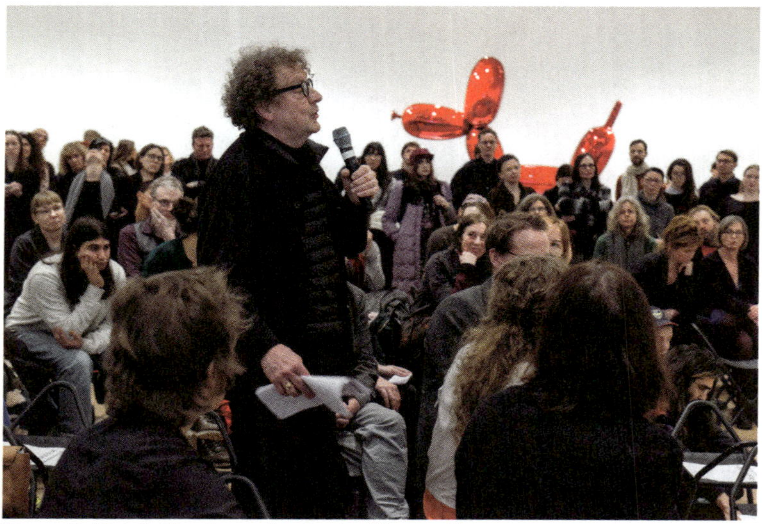

Pierre Guillet de Monthoux developing his question about object-oriented business.

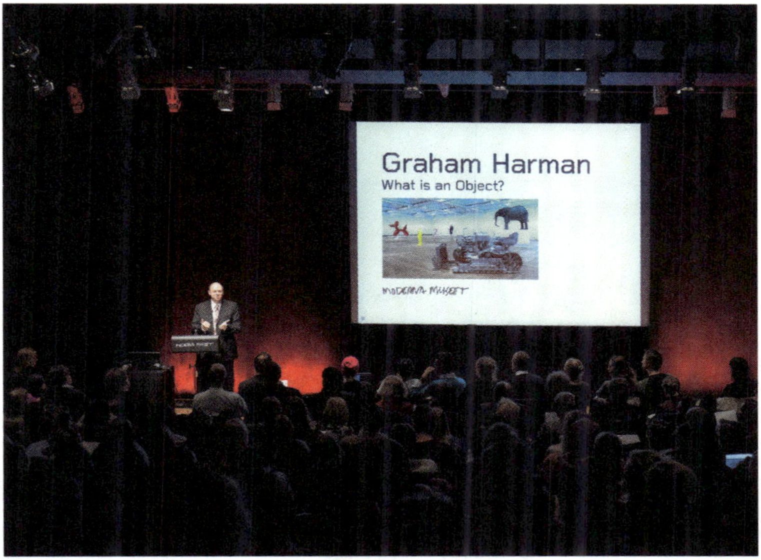

Graham Harman giving his lecture "What Is an Object?"
in a crammed auditorium at Moderna Museet in Stockholm.

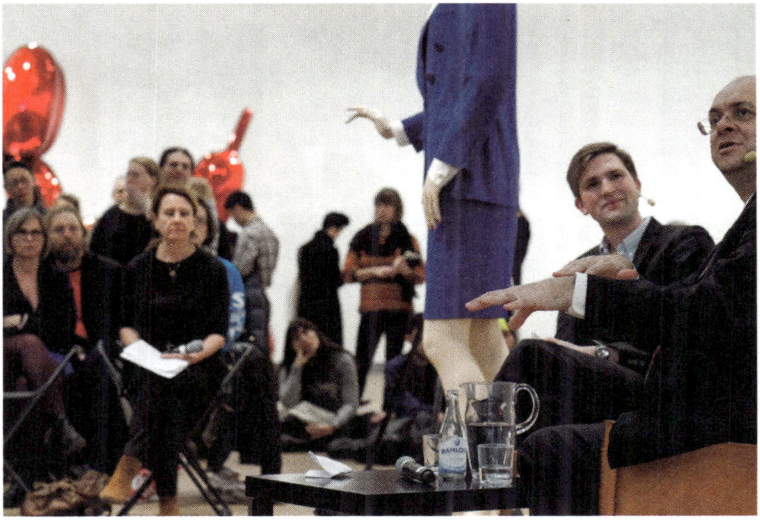

Graham Harman, next to Isak Nilson, answering Erik Wikberg's question
about art as advertising as art.

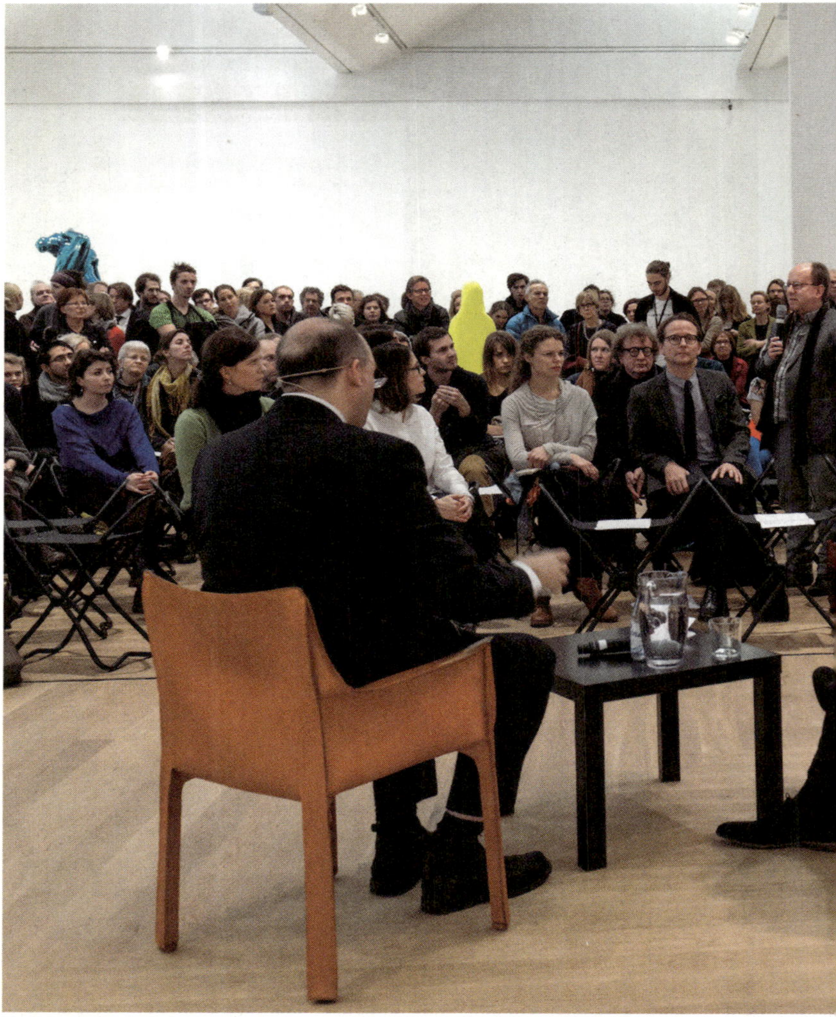

Sven-Olov Wallenstein in a debate with Graham Harman about objects and the subject.

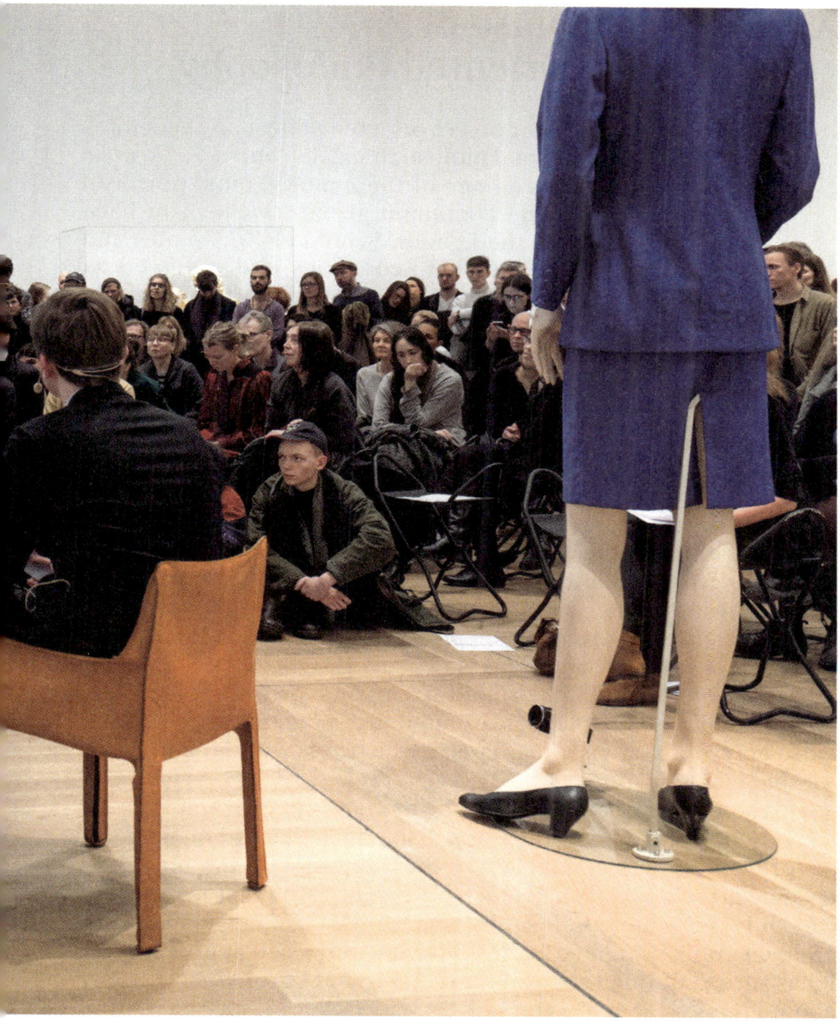

A) The Promise of Object-Oriented Philosophy

ISAK NILSON: Graham, your object-oriented philosophy generates interest far beyond philosophical discourse. *ArtReview* has ranked you as one of the hundred most powerful influences in the contemporary art world. You have been invited to the London School of Economics and the Stockholm School of Economics, and architects as well as scholars of literature use object-oriented philosophy to rethink their disciplines. Why do you think there is this widespread interest, and in which discipline do you think that your object-oriented philosophy holds the greatest promise?

GRAHAM HARMAN: I think the reason the interest has caught on in so many disciplines is because the problem of objects and their relations is so general. Virtually every discipline is already conversant with this theme, and nearly every discipline faces a situation in which relations have had the upper hand for a long time. Take architecture, for example. I was just looking at Patrik Schumacher's *The Autopoiesis of Architecture*, that giant two-volume work, which might be viewed as the retroactive intellectual rationale behind Zaha Hadid Architects' projects.[1] It is very much a relational theory of architecture, claiming that objects exist only in a system of parametric relations, with no autonomy for the individual objects.

So object-oriented philosophy has come at the right time for many people in so many different disciplines that are facing a crisis of over-relationalizing, where the autonomy of the object, in each of these fields, has been lost. I would guess that is probably why object-oriented philosophy is sweeping through so many disciplines. And yes, I have been somewhat surprised at how rapidly it has spread through some of these fields, but I'm obviously happy about it.

Sometimes I am asked, "Do you worry that people will misunderstand?" I don't, because I don't care so much about being understood properly in each discipline. On this point, and few others, I'm a pragmatist. It's important to have a theory that proves fruitful for other disciplines. It seems like architecture may be the furthest along in trying to put this to work, compared with other disciplines. But it's happening in a lot of different places.

Except philosophy! [*Laughter from the audience.*] Philosophy is the slowest field to adopt my ideas. Isn't that funny?

B) Objects in a Digital World

LARS STRANNEGÅRD: At the Stockholm School of Economics, an increasing proportion of our alumni start their own companies. The majority of these companies are digital, in one sense or another, and our students nowadays interact over Facebook, Instagram, et cetera. They even want us to give lectures online. So they want to see and hear the professors, but not necessarily experience them physically.

So, obviously, students live a large proportion of their lives online, and the physical seems to play a different role. And since I am an educator responsible for a school that needs to be in touch with the developments in society and science, my question is how philosophical thoughts actually change when digitalization is increasing and interactions are taking different forms. Are there any philosophical insights that become more important when physical objects and human interaction take on new forms in a more digital world? Or does the increase in digitalization not matter at all for a philosopher like you?

GRAHAM HARMAN: In a sense, it matters a great deal because we are now flooded with objects that are no longer just physical objects. Any object-oriented philosopher in the past would probably have overemphasized the physical at the expense of other things. The word "object" itself has a lot of physical connotations. But now we find ourselves surrounded by so many fictional objects, by images, by all kinds of things that don't count as objects in the old sense. In a way, our world is more populated by these things than it is by traditional physical objects. And in a sense, this encourages one to pursue a wider philosophy that can take

1 Patrik Schumacher, *The Autopoiesis of Architecture, Volume 1: A New Framework for Architecture* (Chichester, UK: Wiley, 2011); Patrik Schumacher, *The Autopoiesis of Architecture, Volume 2: A New Agenda for Architecture* (Chichester, UK: Wiley, 2012).

account of all these various digital images and things. And in artistic terms, I think there is also an implication.

One of my favorite sentences about art came from J. G. Ballard, the recently deceased British novelist.[2] He said that the role of the artist in our times has reversed from what it once was. It used to be that artists were called upon to create fictions. But now, we are surrounded by so many fictions that we need artists to produce realities to hold those fictions together. It's too easy simply to put some strange thing in a gallery and declare it to be an artwork. It is much harder to compel *belief* in that object, with so many of these fictions running rampant.

I also tend to be one of those who think that video games have a bright aesthetic future. Everyone is waiting for the first great artwork to emerge out of the video-game world. I suspect it will happen, though it probably hasn't happened yet.

C) Time, Space, and What an Object Is Not

MICAEL DAHLEN: Thank you very much, Mr. Harman, for a lecture that I loved and that I absolutely hated. I loved the fact that I had so many thoughts running around in my head, and I hated the fact that it made me feel really stupid [*laughter from the audience*]. I have so many questions, and now I'll let you know just how stupid I am.

All these objects in this exhibition got me thinking about time and space. One thing that the objects have in common is that they took a lot of time to produce and they take up a lot of space. These are symptoms of the age we live in, where time is something really valuable—as when you were watching the clock when you were talking, and as I am watching the clock right now, while I am trying to figure out a question—and space—like when everybody was fighting to get into the room downstairs, which a lot of people did ... So could the fact that these objects are huge and took a long time to produce be some sort of symptom of how we value time and space more than ever?

I also thought about objects as art. But I guess art is an object too, and we can never really fully know what an object is. Can we know what an object *is not*? Can one say what art *is not*?

And finally, one more thing that I would like to ask about is life. You talked about components and effects. All these objects, component-wise, are 90 percent identical to all of us. And they have very similar effects on you as I have, like this one [*pointing toward* Fall '91 *(1992) by Charles Ray*], but we say that they are not alive. But still, we cannot really know all the properties and beings of objects. Can we really say that they are not alive, or do we just not realize how alive they are?

So I guess that my question to you would be: Which question should I ask? [*Laughter from the audience.*]

GRAHAM HARMAN: [*Long pause.*] Let me begin with the question of whether we can know what a thing is not. The accusation people sometimes make against my philosophy is that I can only say what objects are not. It, thus, becomes a "negative theology," as people put it, because I am always saying that you can't make any definite paraphrase of an object. An object is always deeper than any literal description of it, and so forth. Now, the funny thing is that the great early practitioner of negative theology was a person whom we now call Pseudo-Dionysius. It was believed that this was the Dionysius mentioned in the New Testament, but now it is believed that he was not really that person, so he (or she) is called Pseudo-Dionysius instead.

I read Pseudo-Dionysius's works on negative theology. And what's interesting about them is that they are not primarily negative but quite often metaphorical. He is not just saying that God is too powerful to talk about, or that God is too great and our human conceptions of greatness are insufficient to describe him. Instead, he says things like: "In a house, the light from all the lamps is completely interpenetrating, yet each is clearly distinct. There is distinction in unity and unity in distinction. When there are many lamps in a house, there is nevertheless a single undifferentiated light, and from all of them comes the one undivided brightness."[3] And that's a very powerful theological metaphor. So it's not just that he is being negative. It's that he is speaking metaphorically and allusively.

2 V. Vale, *RE/Search, nos. 8/9: J. G. Ballard*, 2nd ed. (San Francisco: RE/Search Publications, 1984).

3 Pseudo-Dionysius, *Pseudo-Dionysius: The Complete Works*, ed. Colm Lubheid (Mahwah, NJ: Paulist Press, 1987), 61.

Metaphors are often taken to be a deficient form of language as opposed to straight-out propositional statements. But I would say the opposite. Aristotle already said that the gift for metaphor is the greatest gift, because a person who can produce metaphors can see resemblances that others cannot.[4] I am inclined to believe this, too. That is why I have such cognitive respect for poets: they are saying things that cannot be paraphrased easily, or at all. And what's happened is that the model of true propositional statements found in natural science has outstripped all the possibilities of other truths, such as the aesthetic ones, or the political ones.[5] So I think that metaphorical language needs to be taken more seriously, without just obsessing over the drawbacks of negative language. And yes, we can say what an object is not, but we should go further than that. We can also say metaphorically and positively what an object really is. And this is the true mark of genius, according to Aristotle.

As for time and space, these are not two dimensions that belong in a class by themselves as the structure of the cosmos. Instead, there are four equal dimensions that I call time, space, essence, and eidos, which have to do with four different permutations of the tensions between objects and qualities. *The Quadruple Object* is the book where I talk about this the most so far, but I will be talking about it more in the next year or so, in a different book.

The problems with time and space are really just more specific versions of the problem with objects in general. We were talking about reification earlier [*pointing at Lars Strannegård*]. Reification is usually taken to mean a bad thing—you're turning something into an object that is not really an object. I think that the opposite is just as bad. We might call it "fluxification" or (though I hate puns) "rheification" from the Greek word for "flow": the idea that people are supposed to take objects and turn them into processes of becoming that have no definite shape. This is actually more dangerous. So, for me, reification is where it's at. You should approach themes like time and space and language in terms of objects. The objects' tensions with their qualities are what come first.

D) Traumatized Objects

DANIEL BIRNBAUM: I remember the first time that I heard your name and also the name of some of your colleagues. It was in connection to the last documenta and its curator [Carolyn Christov-Bakargiev], whom I knew a little bit back then. She talked about her exhibition as something that would criticize an anthropocentric perspective. Some very strange comments and quotes of hers were circulating, especially in the German press. She said that the show was also for animals, and she talked about the political rights of strawberries—things that confused everyone. Then she opened the show and talked about the fact that it was not only about stories of human beings but also about the difficult, dramatic stories of objects. She even went so far as to say that some objects (and she presented a selection of strange things in something that she called the "brain") are traumatized. I remember reviewing the show and saying that, a traumatized subject, I kind of know what that is, but a traumatized object—I do not know what it is. Do you think that objects can be traumatized?

GRAHAM HARMAN: It's a hard question. They can certainly be traumatized from the human perspective. And the example I was going to give was when Duchamp's *The Large Glass* (1915–23) was smashed early on, it actually improved the work when the glass was broken, according to many critics. It's often assumed that object-oriented philosophy entails that all objects come to life and have the same sorts of experiences as humans do. I don't think that is the case.

I have talked about Latour's politics a little already [*referring to the lecture earlier that day*], but will talk about it again here. It's often said about Latour that he is bringing objects into politics, and that this is what constitutes his object-oriented politics. Not really, however; or at least, not in the straightforward way that we as readers might think. The way that Latour's politics

4 Aristotle, "Poetics," in *The Rhetoric and Poetics of Aristotle*, trans. W. Rhys Roberts and Ingram Bywater (New York: Random House, 1984), 233–66.

5 This is also among the major ideas of Latour in *An Inquiry into Modes of Existence: An Anthropology of the Moderns*, trans. Catherine Porter (Cambridge, MA: Harvard University Press, 2013).

are object-oriented is that he brings in inanimate objects as *mediators* in the political sphere.

Latour wrote an early work with the primatologist Shirley Strum about her specialty, baboons.[6] What they noticed was that baboons actually have a highly stratified society. In fact, they have more social interaction than we do, in the sense that baboons constantly have to observe, each and every minute, who is on top of the baboon hierarchy in that moment—who is falling, who is rising, whose stock remains roughly the same. And, as Latour writes years later, thank God that we don't have to do this.[7]

Humans stabilize their positions in the social structure using inanimate objects. We have things like names, clothing, wedding rings, bank accounts, identity cards. These are the things that enable humans to wake up each day being pretty sure of who we are, and not having to renegotiate our position in the polis at each and every moment. He says: Thank God when I go to the post office to buy stamps, the man selling me the stamps doesn't complain about his mother-in-law or ask me about my personal life. Because we've learned to alienate each other using our fixed roles through fixed inanimate objects, and it's actually a fortunate thing for us that we have these objects to keep us stabilized socially.

Now, whether objects can be traumatized, in and of themselves, from their own perspective … I'm not quite sure what to say about that. But don't be too quick to assume that object-oriented philosophy is about vitalism. Not necessarily. Some of my critics, including my colleague Quentin Meillassoux, think that I say that all inanimate objects are alive.[8] But that's not what I say. I simply say that the human experience of the world and the experience of two objects smashing together must start out being treated the same way.

We can't assume that there is an ontological difference between the human subject and everything else, which, of course, is opposed to the view of many contemporary philosophers, such as Slavoj Žižek. He happens to think that the human subject is a unique tear in the fabric of the universe, a case in which something has gone terribly wrong. The appearance of the human subject is an ontological catastrophe, he says.[9] I don't see why it should be that way. I don't see why we should be so different *in kind* from everything else.

Of course, it doesn't follow that inanimate objects can do everything that we can do, such as speak, dream, or plan for the future. Now, as for trauma, I wouldn't know where to put it on this list. I wouldn't know whether to say that an object can actually be traumatized. There are certainly times when an object seems to undergo a trauma in a way that disturbs us. But whether the object itself can be traumatized, I still cannot make up my mind about that.

E) The Art Part of Art Objects

JO WIDOFF: I suppose it falls on me to somehow relate what we have been talking about today to the exhibition. I have this concern, and I think you addressed it quite a lot today, regarding whether there is an "art part" inherent in the art object. I am stealing this idea of the art part from one of the artists in the show, Charles Ray, who made a remark about how, when trying to understand an object, it was the art part that he was looking for. In a way, what I'm asking is: Is there one aspect of an art object, or one background, one category, that can never be removed? If we were, for instance, to see Jeff Koons's vacuum cleaners in a major department store,[10] would they still, as an object, have one aspect of art, even though I, as a beholder or as a subject, do not understand them as art?

GRAHAM HARMAN: I'm not against the idea that art can become art through its contextualization. Let's not think about *these* vacuum cleaners here, but think instead about a contemporary vacuum cleaner. If you go to a department store and see a vacuum cleaner, it's unlikely that you would experience it in aesthetic terms. So what is it that makes these vacuum cleaners aesthetic? One of the things, of course, is that they have been placed in a glass case.

6 Shirley S. Strum and Bruno Latour, "Redefining the Social Link: From Baboons to Humans," *Social Science Information* 26, no. 4 (1987): 783–802.
7 Bruno Latour, "On Interobjectivity," *Mind, Culture, and Activity: An International Journal* 3, no. 4 (1996): 228–45.
8 Quentin Meillassoux, "Iteration, Reiteration, Repetition: A Speculative Analysis of the Meaningless Sign" ("The Berlin Lecture"), trans. R. Mackay, first version, unpublished manuscript (2011).
9 Slavoj Žižek, *Less Than Nothing: Hegel and the Shadow of Dialectical Materialism* (London: Verso, 2012). For a thorough discussion of this topic, see Joseph Carew, *Ontological Catastrophe: Žižek and the Paradoxical Metaphysics of German Idealism* (Ann Arbor, MI: Open Humanities Press, 2014).
10 Referring to *New Hoover Convertibles, New Shelton Wet / Drys 5-Gallon Doubledecker* (1981–87) by Jeff Koons.

Another factor, however, is that they are now thirty or so years old, right? All past objects tend to become aesthetic, because their functional part fades into the background, and the visual aspects take the foreground.

There is something inherently aesthetic about these 1980s-era vacuum cleaners. And, of course, I don't think Marcel Duchamp's urinal would have been aesthetic if you had encountered it in a men's restroom. So I'm not opposed to the idea that a certain context can frame something as an art object. I just think that, at a certain point, the art object becomes separate from that context and takes on a new life of its own. Because no object can absorb all of its contexts.

JO WIDOFF: I'm sorry, my question was probably posed badly. I meant if we placed Koons's *actual* art piece, as it looks right now, in a department store, would it retain an inherent art part?

GRAHAM HARMAN: Do you mean placing it there in a glass case?

JO WIDOFF: Yes.

GRAHAM HARMAN: Okay, well, that would already be giving a signal to those encountering it that it is not for sale, that this is not a normal vacuum cleaner.

One of the things I often do when approaching artworks, literary works, jokes, anything of this sort, is to ask myself: How could you make it worse? Because by looking at how you can make an artwork worse, you can gain insight into how it functions. How would you ruin this? [*Pointing at* Balloon Dog (Red) *(1994–2000) by Jeff Koons.*] For some people, it's probably already ruined—I'm sure Michael Fried thinks this is already completely ruined, aesthetically. But how could you ruin it? What if you were to shrink it down to the actual size of a balloon dog, and make it out of an actual balloon? Would it have the same effect? Probably not. What if you were to make it multicolored? What if you had barking sounds coming out of it?

There are lots of things you could do to this artwork to vary it, which might ruin it, and by examining these, we can see what the art part of it is—what is it that makes it work? But these vacuum cleaners had to be decontextualized and defunctionalized to become artworks. Duchamp showed that you can turn an awful lot of things into an artwork, but I don't think you can do that while they are on a department-store shelf. The Brillo box still had to be brought out of the store and put in a gallery context. There are certain things you have to do; not everything is art.

What's essential about art is that there is a certain inwardness or depth that withdraws behind its visible qualities, something that cannot quite be paraphrased. And not all that claims to be art can pass that test. So there is a difference between things that proclaim themselves to be art and things that actually are art. So I would agree with Charles Ray that there is an art part of things, and I do think that you could put that [*pointing at* New Hoover Convertibles, New Shelton Wet / Drys 5-Gallon Doubledecker *(1981–87) by Jeff Koons*] in a department-store context and keep it art, as long as it were in the glass case—but that's already cheating, in a way. Now, if I were to put these particular vacuum cleaners in a store, and somebody ran across them, I think it would blow their mind, because these are obviously very out of date and, therefore, there is something already aesthetic about them. Just as if you would raid your grandparents' basement and go to a party in clothing from the past, there is an aesthetic effect to that.

F) Curating Object Interactions

SIGRID SANDSTRÖM: I am also going to remain here, in this exhibition. Could you elaborate a bit on how you see different autonomous objects relate to or interact with one another? If we look at the sculptures in this room, what is the nature of their interactions? How does this relate to our understanding of and engagement with them? And how does the individual object relate to the exhibition at large?

GRAHAM HARMAN: Very interesting question. Just as I was arguing earlier, I think an artwork is partly unified but also has different elements that can be moved around, and they can interact with each other in different ways. In a sense, a *show* is an object in its own right, and this is part of why curatorship has become such a sexy profession in recent years. I often hear people talk about curators more than they talk about artists. Why is that? It's because they're putting things in new permutations, they're bringing out different aspects of all these individual works. So, in a sense, there is a new object that has been created here precisely by bringing all these objects together. And I think a lot of what happens in the world, as far as new objects being created, is, in fact, a symbiosis of objects.[11]

There is often a debate in philosophy, for example, between two extreme positions. One of them is the question of whether you are always the same person from conception or birth all the way to death, or are you *many*, constantly transforming your identity in different contexts. Yet, somehow, we already know that neither of these options is true. What really is true is that our life mostly goes along on the same old bland continuum, and then, once in a while, there are big changes. You may have five or six big changes throughout your entire lifespan. But these changes do not normally come from sitting alone in your bedroom, brooding about your life and wondering how to change it. Instead, they come from symbiosis with another entity: another person, an institution, a profession …

These are the irreversible moments in our lives—the moment when we choose a certain university to attend, the moment when you become someone's partner, the moment when you change professions … Or maybe just some incredible experience you have, after which, you are not the same person as before. It is about a symbiosis of objects creating new objects. And successful art shows have that effect as well. There are legendary art shows, just as there are legendary architecture shows, bringing objects together in such a way that they resonate with one another in new ways. And then, of course, there are shows that are failures. And when a show fails, why does it fail? Because it was a mere aggregate of individual art objects that were simply assembled in the same space, without opening up anything about the other works.

G) Object-Oriented Business

PIERRE GUILLET DE MONTHOUX: On my way here, I looked at some reviews of this exhibition. They talked about the perfection of the artworks, the technological skills going into them, the extreme problems of finding the right producers, finding the right materials, so the whole technicality of it—the second table, in a sense. And then they dealt with the role of the artist, and the people organizing the whole thing, those who connect the connectors, and the financial side of it, how the art object is a financial kind of innovation. So we are in this world, in the business school, and we know these things. And even someone who has not studied business knows it because they have read the papers and the critics. But if you come in as a new student, or if you are in business, what could you do to resurrect the object, to drive a wedge between the first and the second table, and do something? Some colleagues of mine are arguing that we need to stop talking about the latter, and that we have to go back to the object in the firm, in the company, in manufacturing, and so on. So what is the role of philosophy in trying to do something else than explain advanced technology and the financial skills of the artist?

GRAHAM HARMAN: [*Long pause.*] That's a hard one [*laughter from the audience*]. On the one hand, I don't think philosophy should be giving lessons. Each discipline has its own understanding of how to do things. For example, if an architect invites me to speak, usually the first thing I say is: "Don't expect me to provide any ideas about how to construct buildings, because I have no idea." The problems in philosophy are not the same as the problems in architecture or anything else. I've heard some people in other fields say that the job of philosophy is to make them hallucinate, to make them come up with new ideas that are applicable within their own discipline.

In terms of management, your president [Lars Strannegård of Stockholm School of Economics] has just said that they have been taught for years not to reify a corporation or an institution. I don't read the business literature extensively, but I often hear it said that businesses begin to thrive when they discover what their core mission really is. The example I've often heard is that IBM took a big step forward when they realized that the company wasn't about typewriters, it was about information processing. So they reconceptualized what they did in a deeper way. And these moments of corporations or institutions reinventing themselves do have something of the aesthetic about them.

11 Graham Harman's use of the term "symbiosis" is influenced heavily by that of Lynn Margulis, *Symbiotic Planet: A New Look at Evolution* (New York: Basic Books, 1999).

Concepts like "rebranding" are often condemned as expressions of capitalism in the circles in which I travel, but the idea of a brand is important. This is why I've written, often very defiantly, that I'm very proud of the "speculative realism" brand. Some of the members of that movement reacted very negatively to the name, but a brand helps you cut through information clutter; it helps you get down to what's essential. And I'm pleased by the fact that the name "speculative realism" has caught on.[12] It's never going to do complete justice to the variations and all the different positions that the original members have. But there is a certain aesthetic effect to it because it cuts right to the core of what speculative realism is doing that is new.

It's a realist philosophy, and realism has been out of fashion for over a hundred years in continental philosophy circles. And it's speculative, which, for us, means that ... well, realism is usually boring philosophy. I've often compared it to health inspectors in restaurants. If philosophy is a restaurant, realism is a health inspector who says: "Stop going off on these wild tangents and get down to the real facts! The table is here, a table is a table!"

But we are *speculative* realists because we all have very strange results. In my case, it is the idea that objects can never touch; they have to touch the intermediary and not each other.[13] In Meillassoux's case, his realism involves the idea of a God that doesn't exist but might exist in the future.[14] These are not your grandfather's realisms, which talked about hands existing outside the mind, or tables outside the mind. Mine is actually a very strange kind of realism. But there is a certain aesthetic effect any time you detach an object from whatever qualities we ascribe it. Any time you are thinking and trying to get down to the essence of something, there is something aesthetic about that. But I don't know enough about management schools.

H) Objects and the Subject

SVEN-OLOV WALLENSTEIN: When one speaks about object-oriented philosophy, my normal reaction is that it somehow opposes an overemphasis on the subject. You orient yourself toward the object because there has been from, let's say, the seventeenth century, Descartes, some kind of overemphasis on the subject as being used to constitute the world, to give meaning to the world.

Thus, we have to go back to the object and, as you said, perhaps not entirely erase, but at least minimize, this ontological divide between subject and object.

In your talk, there was a lot of talk about objects. I have some objections to this vague and perhaps indiscriminate use of the term "object." I really don't see the point in calling anything from prime numbers to corporate entities, to Duchamp, to quarks, "objects" in general. I find that not very helpful, but that's not the issue. My real question is that besides this, as it were, thematic, operative talk of objects, there is an implicit talk about subjects: experience, perception, human experience, "No, objects cannot be traumatized, not really." There is always implied some other dimension, which we would traditionally call the subject. But it doesn't really get any attention, any explicit acknowledgment. If everything exists on the same level, if objects relate to objects, still there is some enigmatic field called "experience" and "perception." From where does this come?

GRAHAM HARMAN: As for the talk of the term "objects" being unhelpful, I disagree with that. The problem, if you don't perform that initial flattening move where you treat everything as the same, is that you begin with other commonsensical, inherited ideas of what the different kinds of objects are. You start, for example, by assuming that humans are completely different in kind from everything else that exists.

SVEN-OLOV WALLENSTEIN: Not necessarily—why should I?

GRAHAM HARMAN: Because people do it. People start by assuming that the human subject is radically different in kind from everything else.

SVEN-OLOV WALLENSTEIN: But "people" is vague. Not everyone does that. "People do it" is not an argument. People do a lot of things.

12 Graham Harman, *Speculative Realism: An Introduction* (Cambridge: Polity, 2018).
13 Graham Harman, "On Vicarious Causation," in *Collapse II: Philosophical Research and Development*, ed. Robin Mackay (Falmouth, UK: Urbanomic, 2007), 171–205.
14 Quentin Meillassoux, "Appendix: Excerpts from *L'Inexistence divine*," in *Quentin Meillassoux: Philosophy in the Making*, by Graham Harman, 2nd ed. (Edinburgh: Edinburgh University Press, 2015).

GRAHAM HARMAN: It is an argument, because if a majority of philosophy in our time in the continental tradition is based on the subject, then there is a certain efficacy in challenging that, in saying that we should start by treating everything the same. And, if you're rejecting that, it means that you don't want to make everything the same, as your question indicates. So I think the first move that you have to make, and Latour makes a similar move, is to treat everything in the same way. For him, it's actors—things are treated in terms of their actions. For me, it's that things are treated in terms of their autonomy and their unity with respect to both the parts that they are composed of and the effects that they have. So that's a very powerful opening move, and that's why people object to it, because they don't want to take that step. People want to start by assuming that there is a huge ontological difference between human subjects and everything else.

I don't think that whatever makes humans different needs to be made into a totally different ontological category. There obviously is a difference between humans and other things. Yes, we are more interesting than many of the objects that exist. We are humans ourselves, and so, obviously, we are more interested in humans than we are in other objects. But that doesn't mean that the difference needs to be built into the very foundation of ontology. You say that you don't like the vague term "people." Well, try Descartes, Kant, and Hegel, if those names are good enough for you.

So that's the first step, simply flattening everything else. Now, you can't stay there forever because you need to be able to say different kinds of things about different kinds of objects. Not everything is an artwork; not everything is a human. And I didn't really get the part where you were objecting to the supposedly implicit use of the term "subject" in my lecture, because we know that human experience exists, and there's nothing wrong with talking about human experience and trying to elucidate it. And there's nothing wrong with saying that the human experience of an object is not necessarily different in kind from an object's experience of an object.

Obviously, humans have a different perceptual structure, as far as we can tell, from inanimate objects—inanimate objects might have none at all. But if you boil things down to a more basic category, which is interaction, and say that every interaction fails to exhaust its terms, and that every interaction is a translation, then you can start to look at the difference between humans and physical interactions a bit differently. Because you are starting off by assuming that there is a category called "interaction," which many of these different kinds of things belong to. And then the question of how to rebuild human specificity out of such a theory, how to talk about what makes humans different, emerges again in a different form.

I can't sit here and tell you what I think makes humans different, other than giving the commonsensical examples that we all know: we dream, we plan ahead in the future. But there is no reason to start by assuming that humans are different in kind from other objects. You can, of course, think of it the other way, the naturalist way, and say that humans are not different in kind because everything is built out of small physical particles. But then you are making the opposite mistake, I think, of reducing everything to one basic kind of object: the natural, subatomic.

I) Object-Oriented Philosophy, Money, and Politics

MARCIA CAVALCANTE: During your talk, I was trying to figure out the political implications of your discourse, as you were doing with Latour. And I must say that it seems to me, in part, very dangerous. Because I think what you propose with this general equivalence of everything, in response to Sven-Olov Wallenstein's questions, is a legitimating discourse to neoliberalism. When you say "everything is an object," I would translate this into "everything is money," because you never address the question of what happens when human beings become objects. When mountains, and all other things, become objects. We don't speak about human objects, because then we would have to address the questions of power, of slavery, of control. And this is a very problematic discourse, when we reduce all differences to the general equivalence of money. I think that is what speculative realism provides us with today, and I think that it's very dangerous.

GRAHAM HARMAN: Actually, I would say that we do exactly the opposite, or at least the object-oriented brand of speculative realism does exactly the opposite. If you are saying that everything can be translated into its cash value, what you're doing is looking at the thing from the outside, you're putting a price on the thing, you're converting it into its economic equivalence to something else. This is the opposite of what object-oriented philosophy does because we are saying the object has a depth to it that cannot be translated into a monetary value or any other kind. And if you think of the classic neoliberal statement that the Left complains about, it is surely Margaret Thatcher's infamous claim that "society does not exist." Whereas, for me, society does exist. What exists are not just individual humans as consumers and voters, but society also exists as a larger object in which the smaller, individual objects participate.

My book on Latour's politics is the first explicitly political thing I've ever written.[15] One of my questions was: What is the fundamental distinction in modern political theory? Usually, we get hung up on Left and Right—the Left are the progressives, the Right are the conservatives. Everyone we meet, we try to place them on this spectrum and figure out where on this spectrum they're coming from. While writing the Latour book, it occurred to me that this is not really the basic distinction at work in modern political theory. That basic distinction is actually the one between truth and power. And you will find commitments to truth politics and power politics on both the left and the right.

The truth politics of the Left would simply be the assumption that we already know that all people are equal and that there are certain corrupt class interests or other vested interests that prevent us all from being equal, and therefore, we need to fight these obstacles and destroy them in order to reach the society we desire. Here, I think not only of Marx but also of Rousseau. The truth is known, and we simply have to implement it against all these corrupt interests.

But you also get truth politics from the Right, and I've seen this among the Straussians, who are very influential in America and were especially influential in the George W. Bush administration. The Straussians also think they know the political truth—they simply have an opposite truth from what the Left has. They say that the truth, as Socrates supposedly knew, is that people are not equal and not really improvable. There are certain eternal human types that keep recurring over and over again, and we have to make sure that the best people come out on top.

And so it becomes a rather uninteresting political philosophy, because it simply becomes a question of: How do philosophers survive in the city without being murdered, like Socrates was?

How do we prevent the superior people from being destroyed? But again, this also assumes that we *know* the political truth, and I don't think we do. But I also don't think that politics can be reduced to a simple calculation of power and national interests, as in the Hobbesian or Machiavellian tradition—and even sometimes on the left. With identity politics on the left, you sometimes get the sense that politics is just a power struggle in which our preferred identity group needs to gain more power than it currently has.

So, for me, politics is not just about implementing the truth, or just about a power struggle. It is also about trying to determine what the truth is, and I happen to think that nobody knows that. There are a lot of people today who think they know what the political truth is already, and are ready to act on it, and that's politically dangerous. Even Žižek has recently tried to reverse the usual Marxist formula and says that "maybe today is not the time to try to change the world but instead to step back, precisely to think. What we need today is a materialist reversal of Marx back to Hegel."[16] On one level, that's just typical Žižekian irony, but I think there's something to it. We are too quick to assume that we know what the problem is with the world, politically. We are too quick to assume it's capitalism, but I'm not sure we actually know what the problem is.

J) How to Legitimize a Philosophical Orientation: The Case of Speculative Realism

JENNY LANTZ: As an organizational scholar, I am heavily influenced by sociology, and I am interested in careers and trajectories. I know that you are not a big fan of social constructionism or interpretative approaches, but I am, and I'd like to ask you about your career. There is a famous sociological article by Michèle Lamont called "How to Become a Dominant French Philosopher: The Case of Jacques Derrida,"[17] about the legitimation pro-

15 Graham Harman, *Bruno Latour: Reassembling the Political* (London: Pluto, 2014).
16 Anja Steinbauer, "Interview: Slavoj Žižek," *Philosophy Now* 122 (2017), https://philosophynow.org/issues/122/Slavoj_Zizek.
17 Michèle Lamont, "How to Become a Dominant French Philosopher: The Case of Jacques Derrida," *American Journal of Sociology* 93, no. 3 (1987): 584–622.

cess of the theories of Jacques Derrida. As you know, sociologists don't believe solely in individual talent; they also look at circumstances—the social, institutional, and cultural conditions—under which a phenomenon occurs. Inspired by this article, I am curious about your own reflections on the legitimation process regarding speculative realism. Why do you think it has appealed to such a huge group of people and gained so many followers?

GRAHAM HARMAN: For several reasons. One of them has to do with the fact that the question of objects and relations has secretly been central to so many fields for so long; it just hadn't been put into words yet. That's one thing. Another thing is that speculative realism emerged from a subfield—continental philosophy, the French and German tradition of philosophy—where social constructivist approaches had really had the upper hand for a long time. There hadn't been much talk about reality; everything was about language, power, things of this sort. So I think it was really just time for a change.

I also think the internet played a large role in disseminating these ideas very quickly. These days, any remark I put on my blog is read by thousands of people across the world. At lunch today, there was a discussion, and people were asking me about something I didn't realize I had already said: thoughts that were in my head that I didn't realize I had uttered yet. Someone said, "Oh yes, you've said that," and it was in a lecture that I gave in London last March, which is on YouTube. So we have been blessed but also cursed with this new communication technology that philosophy has never dealt with before.

Derrida and these others did not have the internet at their disposal—partly to their good fortune, I think [*laughter from the audience*]. A lot of bad things happen in the blogosphere. You get into horrible fights with people you've never heard of; there are people picking fights under pseudonyms ... It takes a long time to learn not to respond to these people, but it's too tempting to fight back, and then it gets worse ... But it has been a benefit in terms of being able to communicate in some way with people around the world, in any country where blogs can be read, which excludes China and a few other countries, where these blogs are blocked. But I credit much of it to the technological factor.

I also credit a lot of my own career to the fact that I've been following in Latour's wake. I owe a great deal to Latour's actor-network theory, there are just some modifications that I make in terms of treating objects not as relational (as he does) but as non-relational. And so, in a way, Latour has already carved out a huge interdisciplinary audience that I have been able to take advantage of. My book *Prince of Networks*, about Latour, is my most successful book. And so I certainly owe a lot to the audience that he has created through his own hard work.

So that's how I would go about explaining how we've become fairly well known across the world at a fairly rapid pace.

K) Art as Advertising as Art

ERIK WIKBERG: Objects made by Andy Warhol, and others, have been used both as art and advertising. For example, the Swedish company Absolut Vodka commissioned the painting *Absolut Warhol* (1986), which was both reproduced in magazines, as an advertisement, and circulated in museums as a work of art. Some would say that this is not only an object that is both art and advertising, but also an object that is "art as advertising" or even "art as advertising as art." Based on your theory of ontography, and the real, essential qualities of objects, how would you describe such an object and its extensions?[18]

GRAHAM HARMAN: I don't see any reason to exclude the possibility of any possible object being made art, including advertising. Of course, that's a well-established example already; Warhol has been around for fifty or so years. But generally, some decontextualization is necessary. You're not automatically willing to see a commercial on television, or a billboard, and say that it's art for the simple reason that "everything is art." I don't think that works. There are certain definite points at which a thing *does* become art rather than non-art, and I've tried to argue that it's the tension between the object and its qualities springing forth.

And there are certainly things now that are not considered art that might be considered art in the future, and vice versa. Warhol has shown us how you can make nearly anything into art, and maybe Koons is now the most prominent heir of that tradition.

18 The concept of "ontography" is explained in Harman, *The Quadruple Object* (Winchester, UK: Zero Books, 2011).

Maybe someone will find a way to push it even further. But work has to be done, in each of these cases, to make it art. In Duchamp's case, the urinal itself is not art; it had to be framed in a very specific way to be art, in a specific gallery context. The same with the Brillo box, and the same with the balloon dog. I still think there is always labor that has to be performed to move something from the advertising sphere to the art sphere, and it might not always work just because someone *thinks* it works. But there are advertisements that obviously have a certain aesthetic quality to them. I wouldn't have a problem with a museum of beautiful ads; I can see this as a possibility.

L) Organizational Inertia and Symbiosis

EMMA STENSTRÖM: Being in a business school, I'm really curious to hear if, and if so, how, you think object-oriented philosophy can be used to understand and perhaps think and teach about businesses differently. Could object-oriented philosophy inspire us in a similar, or perhaps different, way as it has inspired the art world? How could I, as a researcher, use it to better understand how organizations work? And could it help my students to see other aspects of their future?

GRAHAM HARMAN: I'd be able to answer this better if I had a better understanding of the current state of research in management, a field I don't know well. But last year, I wrote an afterword for a book on assemblage theory in political science—assemblage theory being the idea that things in politics aren't just simple units, but are made up of many parts.[19] I like that tendency, which I suppose may have spread into management as well. But it's wrong to assume that everything is in flux all the time and that we should de-privilege unities, de-privilege giant institutions, because everything is constantly changing. I'm not so sure that everything is constantly changing. There could even be a new kind of theory called "stability theory," about how everything remains the same no matter how much we try to change it.

Institutions obviously have a certain logic of their own. We had a president who came into the American University in Cairo talking about all kinds of radical changes that were going to be made. But in a certain sense, the inherent logic of the institution blocks many efforts to propose changes, and can even make them difficult or impossible. There is a certain logic to how things work in an institution that you can't usually get rid of without firing hundreds of people, which is impractical, and you end up needing to work with the people you have. So there is more tendency to stability in institutions, more inertia than some of these assemblage theories tend to believe. This might make it harder to create an innovation or harder to change an institution.

Maybe Lynn Margulis's model of symbiosis is what you should look at because I think this is where most real change comes from. Things tend not to change from within but tend to change through symbiosis with some other thing. By combining two things, you multiply the power of both. The famous example is that of the stirrup and the horse, from Deleuze, or McLuhan ... Either Deleuze or McLuhan said this, that the stirrup is really what revolutionized medieval warfare because it allowed the knight to sit stably and hold the lance. It's these symbioses that often make for the most changes. And, again, I don't know how much these themes are already appearing in current management studies, so I can't really comment on how much object-oriented philosophy might change the existing discourse.

M) The Commercial Value of an Art Object and Its Aesthetic Quality

EBBA SJÖGREN: Does the commercial value of an object of art change its aesthetic quality?

GRAHAM HARMAN: [*Long pause.*] That's a hard question. What if this Koons sculpture [*pointing at* Balloon Dog (Red) *(1994–2000) by Jeff Koons*] were financially worthless? We know it's not—it's worth tens of millions of dollars, I've been told. And that makes

19 Graham Harman, "Conclusions: Assemblage Theory and Its Future," in *Reassembling International Theory: Assemblage Thinking and International Relations*, ed. Michele Acuto and Simon Curtis (London: Palgrave Macmillan, 2014), 118–31.

me walk around it with a certain reverence that is not necessarily aesthetic. I walk around it with a fear of bumping into it clumsily, knocking it to the ground. The commercial value of it, is that a quality that really belongs to it?

The classic example in recent art would be Damien Hirst's diamond-studded skull, *For the Love of God* (2007), the whole point of which was to create an artwork that was more valuable as a material object than it could ever possibly be as an artwork. So he's created that tension there, something that is more valuable as a diamond-encrusted object than it is as an artwork. And there's a sense in which many are tempted to respect an artwork more if it fetches more money—and, of course, some people are the opposite, and tend to heap scorn on an artwork that has been sold for a large amount of money. But other than that? Well ... [*pause*].

This may be connected with the question of whether the historical quality of historical monuments changes if greater toil was taken to build them. I live in Egypt, and I've been to the pyramids often. There is something about the majesty of the pyramids that comes from the idea of so many slaves losing their lives, being whipped and forced to push around the blocks, and the requisition of all these supplies. That does affect the sense one has of the pyramids—but not necessarily on an aesthetic level. So my provisional answer is no. I'd also get into more trouble if I say the opposite, that the financial value of the work does affect its aesthetic value ... [*laughter from the audience*].

I would say no, because aesthetics for me is about driving a wedge between the object and its qualities. Would the mere increase in the price of an artwork increase the split between the object and its qualities? I would say no, because all you're really doing is increasing the exchange value of the artwork, by putting a higher price on it, and so you're not really affecting the inherent object character of the artwork. That would be my provisional answer—I reserve the right to change it, once I've thought about it a little bit more. It's a tough question.

Appendix

DANIEL BIRNBAUM is an art critic and curator. He is director of Acute Art, a board member of the Hilma af Klint Foundation, and a contributing editor at *Artforum*. Birnbaum was director of Moderna Museet in Stockholm (2010–19), director of the 53rd Venice Biennale (2009), and held the position as rector of the Städelschule in Frankfurt am Main (2000–10).

MARCIA CAVALCANTE is professor of philosophy at Södertörn University. Her main fields of research include German idealism, hermeneutical phenomenology, ancient philosophy, and contemporary philosophy, with a special interest in the relationship between philosophy, poetry, and arts. Her main philosophical question concerns new temporal and spatial categories to think about the experience of a beginning.

MICAEL DAHLEN is an author and professor of marketing and consumer behavior at Stockholm School of Economics. Dahlen's research revolves around value creation in market communication and consumer behavior. He has produced scientific articles on creativity, innovation, and PR, and is the author of several books, such as *Kaosologi* (2016), based on his experiences of changing forty habits in a year, and *Monster* (2011), describing his encounters with famous serial killers.

PIERRE GUILLET DE MONTHOUX is professor of philosophy and management at Copenhagen Business School and director of SSE Art Initiative, a strategic effort for art and humanities at Stockholm School of Economics. His research interests include the intersection and relation between art, aesthetics, and management. He is the author and editor of numerous scientific articles and books, such as *The Art Firm: Aesthetic Management and Metaphysical Marketing* (2004) and *Aesthetic Leadership: Managing Fields of Flow in Art and Business* (2007).

GRAHAM HARMAN is distinguished professor of philosophy at Southern California Institute of Architecture in Los Angeles. He is the originator of object-oriented philosophy and a central figure in the speculative realism trend in contemporary philosophy. He is the author of numerous books, such as *Art and Objects* (2020),

Object-Oriented Ontology: A New Theory of Everything (2018), *Bruno Latour: Reassembling the Political* (2014), and *The Quadruple Object* (2011).

JENNY LANTZ is an affiliated researcher at Stockholm School of Economics. Her research focuses on the cultural economy and organization of gender. She has written books on trends and organization in fashion and taste and organization in the field of cultural production. Lantz has been associate professor in fashion studies at Stockholm University, associate professor in business administration at Stockholm School of Economics, and a fellow at Harvard Kennedy School, Harvard University.

ISAK NILSON is a research fellow at Stockholm School of Economics. He is a board member of the Friends of Moderna Museet and was founding director of SSE Art Initiative. Nilson is also a strategist and has worked for organizations such as LUMA Arles.

SIGRID SANDSTRÖM is a painter, printmaker, and professor at the Academy of Fine Arts, University of the Arts Helsinki. From 2010 to 2020 she was professor of fine arts at the Royal Institute of Art in Stockholm. Sandström's work has been exhibited in numerous museums internationally, such as Moderna Museet, Stockholm; Nationalmuseum in Stockholm; Mills College Art Museum in Oakland, CA; Contemporary Art Museum Houston; and the Museum of Fine Arts, Houston.

EBBA SJÖGREN is associate professor in accounting at Stockholm Business School. Her present research interests include the role of accounting in experts' decision-making and in the coordination of professional work. Currently, Sjögren investigates evaluation and price formation in markets for in-patient pharmaceutical treatments and decision usefulness of financial reporting information from a behavioral user perspective.

EMMA STENSTRÖM is associate professor and center director for the Center for Arts, Business, and Culture at Stockholm School of Economics. Her research mainly focuses on different cultural fields of production, such as circus, dance, theater, arts, crafts, design, and architecture. She has also studied collaborations between arts and business, artistic interventions in organizations, and cultural entrepreneurship.

LARS STRANNEGÅRD is professor in business administration and leadership and president of Stockholm School of Economics. He has published a large number of scientific articles and books, several with a focus on arts, aesthetics, and business. Strannegård is chairman of Beckmans College of Design in Stockholm, and is a member of the boards of the Swedish Arts Council, the Royal Academy of Engineering Sciences, and the Bergman Estate on Fårö Foundation.

SVEN-OLOV WALLENSTEIN is professor of philosophy at Södertörn University. His research areas include aesthetic theory, with a focus on visual arts and architecture, German idealism, phenomenology, critical theory, and modern philosophies of desire, power, and subjectivity. His recent projects include monographs on Adorno as well as Lyotard and translations of Baumgarten's writings on the foundations of aesthetics.

JO WIDOFF is curator of international art at Moderna Museet, Stockholm. She has curated numerous exhibitions such as "Atsuko Tanaka" (2019–20), with Matilda Olof-Ors; "Louise Nevelson" (2017–18); "Yayoi Kusama" (2016); "Life Itself" (2016), with Carsten Höller and Daniel Birnbaum; and "Sculpture after Sculpture" (2014–15), with Jack Bankowsky.

ERIK WIKBERG is a researcher at Stockholm School of Economics. His research focuses on the organization of cultural production, mainly contemporary art and literature. He has published several books and academic articles and is an active lecturer and consultant for a large number of cultural organizations and companies.

Aristotle. "Poetics." In *The Rhetoric and Poetics of Aristotle*. Translated by W. Rhys Roberts and Ingram Bywater, 233–66. New York: Random House, 1984.

Black, Max. *Models and Metaphors: Studies in Language and Philosophy*. Ithaca, NY: Cornell University Press, 1962.

Bourriaud, Nicolas. *Relational Aesthetics*. Dijon: Les presses du réel, 1998.

Brooks, Cleanth. *The Well Wrought Urn: Studies in the Structure of Poetry*. New York: Harcourt, Brace, and World, 1947.

Callon, Michel and Bruno Latour. "Unscrewing the Big Leviathan: How Actors Macrostructure Reality and How Sociologists Help Them to Do So." In *Advances in Social Theory and Methodology: Toward an Integration of Micro- and Macro-Sociologies*, edited by Karin Knorr-Cetina and Aaron V. Cicourel, 11–32. London: Routledge and Kegan Paul, 1981.

Carew, Joseph. *Ontological Catastrophe: Žižek and the Paradoxical Metaphysics of German Idealism*. Ann Arbor, MI: Open Humanities Press, 2014.

Danto, Arthur. "The Artworld." *Journal of Philosophy* 61, no. 19 (1964): 571–84.

DeLanda, Manuel. *A New Philosophy of Society: Assemblage Theory and Social Complexity*. London: Continuum, 2006.

Dennett, Daniel C. "Quining Qualia." In *Consciousness in Contemporary Science*, edited by Anthony Marcel and Edoardo Bisiach. Oxford: Oxford University Press, 1988.

Descartes, René. *Meditations on First Philosophy*. Translated by Donald Cress. Indianapolis, IN: Hackett, 1993.

Dewey, John. *The Public and Its Problems: An Essay in Political Inquiry*. University Park, PA: Penn State University Press, 2012.

Eddington, Arthur Stanley. *The Nature of the Physical World*. New York: MacMillan, 1929.

Fakhry, Majid. *A History of Islamic Philosophy*. New York: Columbia University Press, 2004.

Fakhry, Majid. *Islamic Occasionalism: And Its Critique by Averroes and Aquinas*. New York: Routledge, 2008.

Fried, Michael. "Art and Objecthood." In *Art and Objecthood: Essays and Reviews*, 148–72. Chicago: University of Chicago Press, 1998.

Greenberg, Clement. *The Collected Essays and Criticism, Volume 1: Perceptions and Judgments, 1939–1944*. Chicago: University of Chicago Press, 1986.

Greenberg, Clement. *The Collected Essays and Criticism, Volume 2: Arrogant Purpose, 1945–1949*. Chicago: University of Chicago Press, 1988.

Greenberg, Clement. *Late Writings*. Edited by Robert C. Morgan. Minneapolis: University of Minnesota Press, 2003.

Guillet de Monthoux, Pierre, and Erik Wikberg, eds. *Economic Ekphrasis: Goldin+Senneby and Art for Business Education*. Berlin: Sternberg Press, 2021.

Harman, Graham. "Art without Relations." *ArtReview*, no. 66 (September 2014): 144–47.

Harman, Graham. *Bells and Whistles: More Speculative Realism*. Winchester, UK: Zero Books, 2013.

Harman, Graham. *Bruno Latour: Reassembling the Political*. London: Pluto, 2014.

Harman, Graham. "Conclusions: Assemblage Theory and Its Future." In *Reassembling International Theory: Assemblage Thinking and International Relations*, edited by Michele Acuto and Simon Curtis, 118–31. London: Palgrave Macmillan, 2014.

Harman, Graham. *Immaterialism: Objects and Social Theory*. Cambridge: Polity, 2016.

Harman, Graham. "A New Sense of Mimesis." In *Aesthetics Equals Politics: New Discourses across Art, Architecture, and Philosophy*, edited by Mark Foster Gage, 49–63. Cambridge, MA: MIT Press, 2019.

Harman, Graham. "On Vicarious Causation." In *Collapse* II: *Philosophical Research and Development*, edited by Robin Mackay, 171–205. Falmouth, UK: Urbanomic, 2007.

Harman, Graham. *Prince of Networks: Bruno Latour and Metaphysics*. Melbourne: re.press, 2009.

Harman, Graham. *The Quadruple Object*. Winchester, UK: Zero Books, 2011.

Harman, Graham. *Quentin Meillassoux: Philosophy in the Making*. 2nd ed. Edinburgh: Edinburgh University Press, 2015.

Harman, Graham. *Speculative Realism: An Introduction*. Cambridge: Polity, 2018.

Harman, Graham. "The Third Table." In *The Book of Books*, edited by Carolyn Christov-Bakargiev, 540–42. Ostfildern, Germany: Hatje Cantz, 2012.

Harman, Graham. *Towards Speculative Realism: Essays and Lectures*. Winchester, UK: Zero Books, 2010.

Harman, Graham. "Undermining, Overmining, and Duomining." In *ADD Metaphysics*, edited by Jenna Sutela, 40–51. Aalto, Finland: Aalto University Design Research Laboratory, 2013.

Harman, Graham. "The Well-Wrought Broken Hammer: Object-Oriented Literary Criticism." *New Literary History* 43, no. 2 (Spring 2012): 183–203.

Heidegger, Martin. "The Origin of the Work of Art." In *Off the Beaten Track*, edited and translated by Julian Young and Kenneth Haynes. Cambridge: Cambridge University Press, 2002.

Heidegger, Martin. *Towards the Definition of Philosophy*. Translated by Ted Sadler. London: Continuum, 2008.

Hobbes, Thomas. *Leviathan*. Oxford: Oxford University Press, 1996.

Hume, David. *A Treatise of Human Nature*. Oxford: Oxford University Press, 1978.

Husserl, Edmund. *Logical Investigations*. Vols. 1–2. Translated by J. N. Findlay. London: Routledge and Kegan Paul, 1970.

Kant, Immanuel. *Critique of Pure Reason*. Translated by Norman Kemp Smith. New York: St. Martin's Press, 1965.

Lamont, Michèle. "How to Become a Dominant French Philosopher: The Case of Jacques Derrida." *American Journal of Sociology* 93, no. 3 (1987): 584–622.

Latour, Bruno. *Facing Gaia: Eight Lectures on the New Climactic Regime*. Translated by Catherine Porter. Cambridge: Polity, 2017.

Latour, Bruno. *An Inquiry into Modes of Existence: An Anthropology of the Moderns*. Translated by Catherine Porter. Cambridge, MA: Harvard University Press, 2013.

Latour, Bruno. "On Interobjectivity." *Mind, Culture, and Activity: An International Journal* 3, no. 4 (1996): 228–45.

Latour, Bruno. *Pandora's Hope: Essays on the Reality of Science Studies*. Cambridge, MA: Harvard University Press, 1999.

Latour, Bruno. *Politics of Nature: How to Bring the Sciences into Democracy*. Translated by Catherine Porter. Cambridge, MA: Harvard University Press, 2004.

Latour, Bruno. *We Have Never Been Modern*. Translated by Catherine Porter. Cambridge, MA: Harvard University Press, 1993.

Leibniz, Gottfried Wilhelm. *Philosophical Essays*. Translated by Roger Ariew and Daniel Garber. Indianapolis, IN: Hackett, 1989.

Lippmann, Walter. *The Phantom Public*. New Brunswick, NJ: Transaction, 1993.

Locke, John. *An Essay Concerning Human Understanding*, Vol. 2. New York: Dover, 1959.

Machiavelli, Niccolò. *The Prince*. Translated by Peter Bondanella. Oxford: Oxford University Press, 2008.

Malebranche, Nicolas. *Dialogues on Metaphysics and on Religion*. Translated by David Scott. Cambridge: Cambridge University Press, 1997.

Margulis, Lynn. *Symbiotic Planet: A New Look at Evolution*. New York: Basic Books, 1999.

Marres, Noortje. "No Issue, No Public: Democratic Deficits after the Displacement of Politics." PhD diss., University of Amsterdam, 2005. http://dare.uva.nl/record/165542.

McLuhan, Marshall. *Understanding Media: The Extensions of Man*. Cambridge, MA: MIT Press, 1994.

Meillassoux, Quentin. "Appendix: Excerpts from *L'Inexistence divine*." In *Quentin Meillassoux: Philosophy in the Making*, by Graham Harman. 2nd ed. Edinburgh: Edinburgh University Press, 2015.

Meillassoux, Quentin. "Iteration, Reiteration, Repetition: A Speculative Analysis of the Meaningless Sign" (a.k.a. "The Berlin Lecture"). Translated by R. Mackay, first version, unpublished manuscript, 2011.

Metzinger, Thomas. *The Ego Tunnel: The Science of the Mind and the Myth of the Self*. New York: Basic Books, 2010.

Perler, Dominik, and Ulrich Rudolph. *Occasionalismus: Theorien der Kausalität im arabisch-islamischen und im europäischen Denken*. Göttingen: Vandenhoeck & Ruprecht, 2000.

Pseudo-Dionysius. *Pseudo-Dionysius: The Complete Works*. Edited by Colm Lubheid. Mahwah, NJ: Paulist Press, 1987.

Qur'an. Salih International translation. http://corpus.quran.com/translation.jsp?chapter=8&verse=17.

Schmitt, Carl. *The Concept of the Political*. Translated by George Schwab. Chicago: University of Chicago Press, 2007.

Schumacher, Patrik. *The Autopoiesis of Architecture, Volume 1: A New Framework for Architecture*. Chichester, UK: Wiley, 2011.

Schumacher, Patrik. *The Autopoiesis of Architecture, Volume 2: A New Agenda for Architecture*. Chichester, UK: Wiley, 2012.

Shapin, Steven, and Simon Schaffer. *Leviathan and the Air-Pump: Hobbes, Boyle, and the Experimental Life*. Princeton, NJ: Princeton University Press, 2017.

Simondon, Gilbert. *L'individuation à la lumière des notions de forme et d'information*. Grenoble: Jérôme Millon, 2005.

Stanislavski, Konstantin. *An Actor's Work*. Translated by Jean Benedetti. London: Routledge, 2010.

Steinbauer, Anja. "Interview: Slavoj Žižek." *Philosophy Now* 122 (2017). https://philosophynow.org/issues/122/Slavoj_Zizek.

Strauss, Leo. *Natural Right and History*. Chicago: University of Chicago Press, 1953.

Strum, Shirley S., and Bruno Latour. "Redefining the Social Link: From Baboons to Humans." *Social Science Information* 26, no. 4 (1987): 783–802.

Vale, V. *RE/Search, nos. 8/9: J. G. Ballard*. 2nd ed. San Francisco: RE/Search Publications, 1984.

Whitehead, Alfred North. *Process and Reality*. New York: Free Press, 1978.

Žižek, Slavoj. *Less Than Nothing: Hegel and the Shadow of Dialectical Materialism*. London: Verso, 2012.

This book was made possible by Lena and Per Josefsson, Elisabeth and Martin Wiwen-Nilsson, Ragnar Söderberg Foundation, Stiftelsen Längmanska kulturfonden, Handelsrådet, the Swedish Arts Council, the Culture Administration of the Stockholm County Council, and a wide range of municipal cultural administrations in the Stockholm region. A warm thank-you is extended to them for their generous support. Furthermore, a big thank-you is due to Graham Harman, Katharina Fritsch, Jeff Koons, Charles Ray, Daniel Birnbaum, Lars Strannegård, Marcia Cavalcante, Sven-Olov Wallenstein, Pierre Guillet de Monthoux, Jo Widoff, Sigrid Sandström, Micael Dahlen, Emma Stenström, Jenny Lantz, Ebba Sjögren, Sara Arrhenius, Karin Malmquist, and Lars Ågren.

"Sculpture after Sculpture," 2014–15, with Katharina Fritsch, Jeff Koons, and Charles Ray was curated by Jack Bankowsky (curator) and Jo Widoff (assistant curator). The events "What Is an Object?" and "Thirteen Questions about the Object to Graham Harman" at Moderna Museet in Stockholm on January 16, 2015, were curated by Daniel Birnbaum, Isak Nilson, and Karin Malmquist. Nilson moderated the event "Thirteen Questions about the Object to Graham Harman."

This publication is part of the SSE Art Initiative series Experiments in Art and Capitalism.

Artful Objects:
Graham Harman on Art and the Business of Speculative Realism

Edited by Isak Nilson and Erik Wikberg

Experiments in Art and Capitalism
Volume 1

Series Editors: Pierre Guillet de Monthoux, Isak Nilson, Erik Wikberg
Copyediting: Sarah Stephenson
Proofreading: Isabella Ritchie
Design: Ronnie Fueglister
Printing: Tallinn Book Printers

ISBN 978-3-95679-524-4

Distributed by The MIT Press, Art Data, and Les presses du réel

SSE Art Initiative
Stockholm School of Economics
PO Box 6501
SE–113 83 Stockholm
www.hhs.se/artinitiative

Sternberg Press
Caroline Schneider
Karl-Marx-Allee 78
D-10243 Berlin
www.sternberg-press.com

Sternberg Press

p. 44, top: Jeff Koons, *Balloon Dog (Red)*, 1994–2000. © Jeff Koons; Charles Ray, *Fall '91*, 1992. © Charles Ray; Katharina Fritsch, *Frau mit Hund / Woman with Dog*, 2004. © Katharina Fritsch. Photo: Åsa Lundén / Moderna Museet

p.44, bottom: Jeff Koons, *Balloon Dog (Red)*, 1994–2000. © Jeff Koons; Charles Ray, *Fall '91*, 1992. © Charles Ray; Katharina Fritsch, *Frau mit Hund / Woman with Dog*, 2004. © Katharina Fritsch. Photo: Åsa Lundén / Moderna Museet

p. 45, top: Charles Ray, *Fall '91*, 1992. © Charles Ray; Katharina Fritsch, *Frau mit Hund / Woman with Dog*, 2004. © Katharina Fritsch / Bildupphovsrätt 2019. Photo: Åsa Lundén / Moderna Museet

p. 45, bottom: Katharina Fritsch, *Elefant/Elephant*, 1987/2009. © Katharina Fritsch. Photo: Åsa Lundén / Moderna Museet

p. 46, top: Photo: Åsa Lundén / Moderna Museet

p. 46, bottom: Jeff Koons, *Balloon Dog (Red)*, 1994–2000. © Jeff Koons. Photo: Åsa Lundén / Moderna Museet

p. 47, top: Jeff Koons, *Balloon Dog (Red)*, 1994–2000. © Jeff Koons; Charles Ray, *The New Beetle*, 2006. © Charles Ray; Katharina Fritsch, *Madonnenfigur / Madonna Figure*, 1987. © Katharina Fritsch; Katharina Fritsch, *Frau mit Hund / Woman with Dog*, 2004. © Katharina Fritsch; Charles Ray, *Fall '91*, 1992. © Charles Ray; Charles Ray, *Tractor*, 2005. © Charles Ray; Katharina Fritsch, *Elefant / Elephant*, 1987/2009. © Katharina Fritsch. Photo: Åsa Lundén / Moderna Museet

p. 47, bottom: Jeff Koons, *Balloon Dog (Red)*, 1994–2000. © Jeff Koons; Charles Ray, *Fall '91*, 1992. © Charles Ray. Photo: Åsa Lundén / Moderna Museet

pp. 48–49: Jeff Koons, *Metallic Venus*, 2010–12. © Jeff Koons; Katharina Fritsch, *Madonnenfigur / Madonna Figure*, 1987. © Katharina Fritsch; Jeff Koons, *Michael Jackson and Bubbles*, 1988. © Jeff Koons; Charles Ray, *Fall '91*, 1992. © Charles Ray. Photo: Åsa Lundén / Moderna Museet